Big
Act
**Small**

Working at Collaborative
Ministry through Parish
Pastoral Councils

Johnny Doherty CSsR, Oliver Crilly, Frank Dolaghan, Paddi Curran

*First published 2005 by*
Veritas Publications
7/8 Lower Abbey Street
Dublin 1
Ireland
Email publications@veritas.ie
Website www.veritas.ie

ISBN 1 85390 995 5

Bible texts are taken from the *Jerusalem Bible*, Darton, Longman & Todd, London.
We are indebted to Fr Michael McGoldrick and the Carmelite Community of Avila,
Dublin, whose hospitality made it possible to finish the book.

Designed by Bill Bolger
Printed in the Republic of Ireland by Betaprint, Dublin

*Veritas books are printed on paper made from the wood pulp of managed forests. For every
tree felled, at least one tree is planted, thereby renewing natural resources.*

To Fr Chuck Gallagher SJ
whose vision for the Church
has inspired us and many others

# Contents

**Fr Johnny Doherty** is a Redemptorist who has worked as a specialist with Accord, directed Veritas Parish Renewal Resources in the 1970s and early 80s, author of *Living the Sunday Liturgy; Do You Want to be Well Again?; A Movement of Continuous Prayer for Marriage & Family Life; Together Forever* – a set of videos on marriage. He is currently Rector of the Community in Esker, Athenry, Co. Galway.

**Fr Oliver Crilly** is Parish Priest of Ardmore, Derry. He was formerly Director of the Catholic Communications Institute of Ireland. Two of his recent publications are: *Is it about a Bicycle?* – a series of Thoughts for the Day – and *A Shortcut to the Gospels*. He is at present Vice-Chairperson of NCPI. Both he and Fr Johnny are involved with the Bishops' Commission for Pastoral Renewal and Development.

**Paddi Curran** is a single person with lifelong involvement in her parish and several years' experience in the Esker Retreat House and Youth Village, Athenry. As Parish Secretary in Ardmore she has been involved in the process of parish development and in shaping the material for *Think Big, Act Small*.

**Frank Dolaghan** is married to Aileen, and with her is a co-founder member, with Fr Johnny Doherty, of The Love is for Life Trust. He is a consultant in Strategic Planning, through his company Mentor Economic Development Ltd, and has been a pioneer in applying the principles of Strategic Planning and Leadership to local community and parish development.

## About the book

We would love to tell you that this book is the answer to your prayers, that you will find here the method that will solve all your problems about parish development, collaborative ministry and forming and running your parish pastoral council. The desire for the one stop shop for pastoral and personal renewal is as old as the young man in the Gospel who asked Jesus: 'What (one) thing must I do to inherit eternal life?'

The reality is not so simple. What you have here is an example of a different approach: instead of a blueprint, this is more like a narrative. It is the story of some people's experience of working at parish development, with their attempt to put on paper the ideas and processes which lie behind the efforts to expand the boundaries of possibility in living the life of a parish community in the twenty-first century.

The title, *Think Big, Act Small*, says the same thing in a slightly different way. *Think Big* implies a vision, looking beyond where we are now to future possibilities, and looking beyond the boundaries of our own parish to the wider mission of the Church. *Act Small* is an acknowledgement of the limitations of our people and place. On the one hand, whatever we do is likely to be incomplete and untidy, so that we may wonder if it was worth the effort. On the other hand, any small step that we take is significant. The greatest achievements are built little by little. It is the spirit of persistence, placing one little effort on top of another, which achieves results in the long run.

The narrative approach has the advantage of flexibility. One person's story stimulates another person to reflect on their story. Elements of this book may apply in different ways in different situations. The process has a particular application to a parish beginning to look at renewal and development and the formation of a pastoral council. But where a pastoral council or similar body already exists, strategic planning, partnership and encouraging a shared approach to leadership are equally relevant. The key is to trust in God's Spirit working through us in our own situation.

That is why Part Two of the book is so important. Reflection on the Scriptures is at the very heart of the process of development and renewal in parishes. The word of God in the Scriptures is the main source for our vision, and the continuing nourishment on the journey of exploration as we stretch the boundaries of possibility.

In the book, for practical reasons, the Scripture reflections are placed together after the description of the development process and the thinking behind it. In reality, the Scripture passages were used from the very beginning of the process: in the Parish Mission, in the first Parish Assembly, during the training and induction of the Pastoral Council, and in all kinds of meetings. A lot of the inspiration and excitement flowed from the Scriptural sources, and shaped what followed. The Scriptures are the daily bread of a community which seeks to be led by the Spirit of God.

One Scripture passage had a particular resonance for the theme of *Think Big, Act Small*. The Marriage Feast of Cana is relevant, not just for wedding liturgies, but for the Church's life in the risen Christ, for persevering prayer, for our Lady's advice: 'Do whatever he tells you', and for the value of our own contribution, however little. The six water jars become a symbol: we play our part by filling them to the brim, trusting that Jesus will do the rest. That is why the water jars appear on the cover of the book. Their message is the same as that of the title. Do your best. Do what you would do if you weren't afraid. Jesus will turn the water into wine, and his disciples will believe in him.

# Foreword by Martin Kennedy

In a letter at the turn of this century Pope John Paul II called on local churches across the world to move. To 'put out into the deep'. His image suggests powerfully that we leave the safe confines of the harbour of routine pastoral practice in a commitment to bringing the gospel to the people of the twenty-first century. This does not involve an essentially new programme for the Church. The gospel message is the same as ever. 'It has its centre in Christ himself, who is to be known, loved and imitated.' But the changing circumstances require that the pastoral methods we use be adapted to the circumstances of each community. 'I therefore earnestly exhort the Pastors of the particular churches, with the help of all sectors of God's people, to plan the stages of the journey ahead' (*At the Beginning of the New Millennium*, page 29).

This culture of pastoral planning, of reaching out beyond what is familiar, is clearly a source of much anxiety in our Church. Many of us, formed by a rigid, self-satisfied pastoral system, understandably find it perplexing to be asked to move into new ways of working. Tasks like collaboration and evangelisation, at the centre of John Paul's challenge, seem to be calling us out into unsafe, choppy waters. In the context of our very changed society we don't feel confident. We don't feel up for it.

I believe the core pastoral challenge facing all of us in these circumstances is to nurture in our hearts a sense of hope. A sense of hope that the gift of the gospel can be offered and received in our twenty-first century culture. A sense of hope that all of us involved in Church ministry – laity, priests, religious and bishops – have the capacity, if we work together, to be effective ministers of the gospel. It is this hope that will give us heart. It is heart that will give us the courage to move.

This book offers hope and heart in two ways. In the first place it is not a prescription about what we should be doing. Rather it is a description of how one parish has already moved to respond to the challenge of collaborative mission. That is the 'Act Small' part of the book. A detailed account, warts and all, of the journey undertaken by Ardmore parish in Derry since the turn of the Millennium. A journey that is of course on-going and incomplete. The core of the journey is a simple process by which the parish community mandated the Parish Pastoral Council to act on a range of pastoral priorities, and how the Council in turn engaged the community in the actions. And what is very interesting is that the stages of the journey all have a familiar ring. Parish mission, parish survey, parish assemblies, pastoral council, working groups, training, planning, action, evaluation. Even though the journey is into uncharted territory none of the stages are beyond us. And the emphasis throughout is not on performance and perfection, but on participation.

A second source of hope and heart in this book is the account it gives of the vision that inspired the movement. This is the 'Think Big' part. Offered here in a highly accessible and deeply attractive manner is an overview of the good news of the gospel for today's world, and the implications of this good news for today's parishes. And what the authors communicate so well is a sense of joy in that good news, a joy that transforms the challenge of evangelisation from a fearful burden into a delightful adventure. As one person who has had the pleasure of meeting and working with them I am constantly struck by their sense of humour. Their ability to take their task of evangelisation seriously without remotely becoming serious about themselves. Their ability to face the reality of evil in the world without becoming depressed and de-energised. That's a beautiful gift to have in ministry today and this book shows the deep roots of that humour in their grasp of the good news. They have a deep sense of God's encouraging word and supportive presence in the Scriptures, in our Church tradition, and in the world today. There is throughout a sense of fidelity to and love for the Church. And in this fidelity there is freedom to hold up in a

*'Be not afraid.'*

critical light Church practices and culture that limit our effectiveness in communicating the good news of the gospel.

There are many parishes that are embarking on this journey 'into the deep'. All of them, in their own way, offer very valuable signposts for the journey. In this respect Ardmore is not very different or very special. But what is special is the trouble the parish has taken to put together a very meticulous, detailed account of its journey and the inspiration that motivated it. Not so that we should follow in every detail, but so that we can have a clear sense that the journey is possible. For all of us who are fearful of new journeys, it is very good news to be able to hear the account of some who have gone ahead of us and are now reporting back. 'Be not afraid' is their message.

# Introduction

The exploration and reflection which is developed in this book had its starting point in the year 2000. In a sense, then, it is rooted in the Millennium experience, in the celebration of 2000 years of Christianity. At its centre is the person of Jesus Christ.

The great formative event of the twentieth century in the life of the Catholic Church was the Second Vatican Council. We have based our process on the insights of the Council. Of particular relevance is the articulation of the status and role of the laity in the Church as expressed before, during and after Vatican II. (See for example *Christifideles Laici*.)

As well as this underlying policy direction of the Church, based on the theology of Vatican II, the processes documented here take their origin from specific pastoral challenges facing the Church at the beginning of the new millennium. The immediate context of these challenges is change in the Church: change in patterns of practice, change in the culture both of the Church itself and of society, loss of morale because of the prevalence and mishandling of cases of child sexual abuse, and the significant reduction in numbers of clergy and religious, on whom dioceses and parishes used to depend – probably to an unhealthy degree – for pastoral services and pastoral initiatives.

While these changes and challenges create the context of pastoral exploration, pastoral development of the kind we are discussing is more deeply rooted in the nature of the Church itself. The Church is a community, a pilgrim people, but also the body of Christ, united in him. The living reality of the Church and all the activity of the Church flows from that. If the Church Community is to act effectively, it must act together. That is not just a practical conclusion: it is the whole spirituality and ethos of the Church, and it has significant implications for leadership in the Church.

Bishops and priests have a very specific role in leadership in the Church. But that role is not to be exercised in isolation. It cannot be exercised in isolation. To gather God's people, to work in the power of the Spirit, means working together, in what the Vatican Council called the spirit of collegiality. It means forming a community which is led by the Spirit, after the model of the early Church described in the Acts of the Apostles. The whole community should be involved in prayer, discernment and action, because 'the Holy Spirit works in the world through the hearts of all who believe' (*Opening Prayer of the Mass of Pentecost Sunday*).

In the following pages we describe a process where the leadership of Ardmore Parish:

1. Sought to expand the boundaries of possibility, 'opening wide the doors to Christ' from the introductory parish mission in May 2000.

2. Consulted the community of the parish, initiating their involvement and inviting everyone to be part of the process of parish development.

3. Began to develop infrastructures involving parishioners first in a Parish Assembly and then in a Parish Pastoral Council and associated working groups.

At the Parish Assembly in October 2000 parishioners drafted a vision statement, indicating that we wanted Ardmore to be a parish where:

- people come first;

- everyone who wants to be involved can be involved;

- everyone feels valued and welcomed;

- priests and people work in partnership;

- we have the courage to invoke change;

- we care for everyone;

- young people play an active role;

- our faith is strong and vibrant;

- we have good relationships with other Churches.

# Part One
# It is wonderful for us to be here

# A Process for Parish Development

## 1. SHARED LEADERSHIP AND RESPONSIBILITY

Parish Pastoral Councils should by now be taken for granted as the normal infrastructure of any parish where there is an effort to involve people in the development of parish life. The theory has been widely explored and written up. Collaborative ministry is not just an emergency measure to deal with the growing shortage of priests. It is of the nature of the Church. It is a spirituality, as the Abbé Micheneau pointed out in France in the 1940s, and as Pope John Paul II underlined in *Novo Millennio Ineunte in* 2001:

> The spirituality of communion, by prompting a trust and openness wholly in accord with the dignity and responsibility of every member of the People of God, supplies institutional reality with a soul (par. 45).

> The Church of the Third Millennium will need to encourage all the baptised and confirmed to be aware of their active responsibility in the church's life (par.46).

The underlying theology is clear: the Holy Spirit works in the world through the hearts of all who believe. The challenge is to provide the Holy Spirit with a forum, to create basic structures which will enable the Holy Spirit to work in our parish through the hearts of those who believe. That includes the priest or priests, but it also includes the 'lay faithful', the *Christifideles Laici*.

> The parish is, first, a people. It can be called an expression of the communal, ecclesial character of Catholic Christian life. But, simply stated, it is a people, a people called together by God. It is a people empowered by the Spirit to make increasingly true and obvious their response to God through Christ. The Parish tries to take shape in this context of faith and prayer, always with openness to the Spirit. (United States Catholic Conference: Committee on the Parish, 1980, paragraph 9.)

The experience of life in a parish is about spiritual and pastoral growth and development. A parish is a people, part of the community we call Church, living and working together, celebrating Mass and the sacraments, welcoming new members, rejoicing with those celebrating Baptism and Confirmation and with those getting married, and standing in solidarity with those who suffer from illness, accident or bereavement.

## Bounded by routine

*'Recognising the enormity of the task we have and the wonder of that task. Then each of us takes our own place fully in accomplishing that task, the transformation of our world.'*

Yet the life of a parish can often be bounded by routine. It can seem to be enough to manage the morning Mass, the weekly Confessions, the hospitals, the needs of schools and traditional adult groups and devotions. Peripheral activities for the priest, like signing passport forms or driving licence applications, can even seem to justify structures and support systems, so that the first priority is maintenance: keeping things as they are, as they always have been in our time.

Of course there is also the routine of parishioners' lives: the demands of rearing a young family, the pressures of work, the competing interests of sport and many voluntary community activities. Parishioners also have fixed routines in the way they have lived their faith over many years.

One of the things which prevents development and renewal in parish life is fear of change. Fear of change affects both priest and people. It takes courage and creativity to move forward, to initiate change and development. The best-selling book *Who Moved my Cheese?* includes the pertinent question: 'What would you do if you were not afraid?'

## Learning from others

However, it is no longer a question of setting out into the unknown. There are many examples of work in progress in parishes and dioceses. We can learn from each other, from the experience of success and from the experience of failure. Parish development is a long-term project. The Archdiocese of Dublin has been working on a process of parish renewal and development since 1985; when Archbishop Kevin McNamara set up a committee to explore possibilities, the first survey came up with four priorities: lay participation, adult faith formation, renewal of priests, and youth ministry.

Development and renewal in parishes involves:

1.  The renewal of the priesthood as a vocation to leadership;

15

2. The gathering of the people of the Church into being a family for the Father, and not just people who have religion;

3. The choosing and commissioning of leadership among this family for the building up of the whole Body;

4. The training of this leadership among the people in such a way that new leadership is always being created.

The emphasis on leadership is a key part of the picture. It is no longer about the leadership of the priest in isolation. It is about shared leadership. It is about the identification and formation of women and men who will take on a shared responsibility for the future of the parish.

**Official Policies**

Not only can we learn from situations where this kind of leadership is already happening. It is also supported by the official policies of the Catholic Church at the highest level. The Second Vatican Council's *Decree on the Ministry and Life of Priests* describes the leadership of the priest in these terms:

> 'In the name of the bishop they gather the family of God as a community enthusiastically striving towards unity, and lead it in Christ through the Spirit to God the Father.' (Par 6.)

*The Decree on the Apostolate of the Laity* states:

> The lay faithful should accustom themselves to working in the parish in close union with their priests, bringing to the Church community their own and the world's problems as well as questions concerning human salvation, all of which need to be examined together and solved through general discussion. As far as possible the lay faithful ought to collaborate in every apostolic and missionary undertaking sponsored by their own ecclesial family. (Vatican II: *Decree on the Apostolate of the Laity*)

Pope John Paul II, in *Christifideles Laici*, comments:

> The Council's mention of examining and solving pastoral problems 'by general discussion' ought to find its adequate

and structured development through a more convinced, extensive and decided appreciation for 'Parish Pastoral Councils' on which the Synod Fathers have rightly insisted.

That is not a vague or ambivalent statement. Pope John Paul II called for a more convinced, extensive and decided appreciation for Parish Pastoral Councils. He linked his call to the Decree on the Apostolate of the Laity (Vatican II, 1965). In 1983 the new Code of Canon Law included provision for diocesan and parish pastoral councils. More recently, in 2001, at the beginning of the new millennium, Pope John Paul again emphasised that 'the Church will need to encourage all the baptised and confirmed to be aware of their active responsibility in the Church's life' (*Novo Millennio Ineunte, par 46*). Against that background, how is it that there is not a pastoral council in every diocese and in every parish throughout the country?

Following Vatican II, the Catholic Bishops' Conference in Ireland established a number of commissions and advisory bodies at national level (1969 and early 1970s), including the Council for the Laity. The Council for the Laity produced guidelines for setting up parish councils, and a booklet was published by Veritas and distributed widely. Many parishes took up the challenge and established parish councils.

There was an energy around, in the aftermath of Vatican II, for doing new things. Parish priests saw in parish councils a genuine opportunity for involving lay people in the life of the Church. Committed lay people enthusiastically welcomed the opportunity to be involved. Quite a number of parish councils made a significant contribution to the organisation and development of their parishes.

But something went wrong. Just a few years after the initial launch of parish councils, and poignantly by the time the new Code of Canon Law was recommending them in 1983, many of the early parish councils had ceased to exist, or had ceased to function effectively.

The initial enthusiasm had not been matched by training and experience. In the absence of an appropriate church model for interaction and management, parish council members, including the parish priest, borrowed heavily from the procedures of business meetings or local political groups. These procedures were based on an adversarial model: I had my agenda, I argued my case against yours, I formed alliances, and when there was not agreement on the way forward, I appealed to a majority vote. This model may have worked in many instances, because of genuine good will and friendship. But in many parishes the time came when a majority vote of parish council members came into conflict with the parish priest's responsibility under Canon Law and diocesan policy. If the parish priest yielded, he would be in trouble for not carrying out the role to which he had been appointed. Many areas of Church life and discipline in any case fell outside the remit of his or the parish council's powers. From the perspective of the new parish council, the members didn't appreciate being told that their vote and their voice was merely consultative, and the parish priest was under no obligation to act on it. The fact that this was clearly stated in the Code of Canon Law (Canon 536, paragraph 2) was little comfort to them. They may have suspected, sometimes rightly, that the parish priest was extending the protection afforded to him by the Code of Canon Law to cover matters of his own personal preference, rather than of any higher authority.

In this kind of conflict, the outcome was often that the parish council was discontinued, or that while it remained in existence in theory, in practice no further meetings were called. The Code of Canon Law stated that the parish council, being advisory to the parish priest, ceased to exist when the parish priest died or was transferred. If difficulties, or even the rumour of difficulties had existed, the new parish priest didn't have to take any positive action; all he had to do was not to set up a new parish council.

The Code of Canon Law in 1983 used the term 'pastoral council' both for diocese and for parish. This term 'pastoral' has provided the basis for re-thinking and for re-visioning the parish 'pastoral' council, and for distancing the new generation of pastoral councils from the sometimes difficult experiences of the past.  Some parishes have tried to achieve this distance by using terms like 'core group', or by creating a composite parish assembly structure with a 'committee'. While this is understandable, there is a lot to be said for adopting the official terminology of the Code of Canon Law, and clarifying the parameters and functions of a pastoral council, and in particular, establishing a different model from the business/political adversarial model. The new model which has achieved widespread acceptance is a consensus model, where decision-making is based on a shared seeking of God's will and the guidance of the Spirit. *Revisioning the Parish Pastoral Council* (Paulist Press, 2001) gives this useful, if somewhat oversimplified table of comparisons between the older 'parish council' and the newer 'parish pastoral council':

| From | To |
| --- | --- |
| Parish Council | Parish Pastoral Council |
| A Body of Leaders | A Leadership Body |
| Co-ordinating Ministries | Articulating the Mission |
| Crisis Management | Pastoral Planning |
| Doing Activities | Empowerment and Oversight |
| Business and Politics | Prayer and Discernment |
| Competition | Collaboration |
| Voting | Consensus |

*Learning a process of shared leadership.*

Using the term 'pastoral' also underlines that the pastoral council's responsibility is for the overall spiritual and pastoral development of the parish. When a parish priest is appointed by the bishop of the diocese, he is given responsibility for both the administrative and pastoral care of the parish. Usually he will involve lay people in both of these areas: people with relevant management and financial skills to support him and work with him in administration, especially in the finance committee, and people with other skills and commitment to participate in reflection and planning for the spiritual and pastoral needs. It is unhelpful to confuse these two areas. It is also unhelpful to separate them totally: it is tempting to say that lay people with particular skills will look after the administration, leaving the priest free to look after the spiritual needs like Mass and the Sacraments, prayer, personal support and counselling. In fact, all these areas are interconnected: financial budgeting, for example, is simply quantifying in pounds or Euro what pastoral action will cost. The cheque book will reflect the priorities of parish life. What is needed is not separate spheres of leadership, but learning a process of shared leadership in which priest and people together can collaborate in building the kingdom of God in this local faith community.

Over the last twenty-five years, the most successful efforts at development and renewal in Irish parishes happened when the programmes were 'faith led' – that is, when it wasn't just a matter of organising people in a tidy and efficient way, but there was a real openness to the Spirit, and people worked together in the context of prayer and Scripture to discern where the Holy Spirit was leading their parish community.

Where people are genuinely led by the Spirit, they will not seek their own fulfilment, rather they will seek what is best for others, for their parish, for the Church and for the world.

There's a fifteenth century Russian icon of The Descent of the Holy Spirit on the Apostles. It shows the apostles gathered in a kind of horseshoe formation, leaving a space at the bottom centre of the picture. At the top the Holy Spirit descends as tongues of flame. The apostles hold scrolls representing the Word of God. There is a solemn atmosphere, a sense of expectation. In the space at the bottom centre there is a dark doorway, framing a little man who waits with hands held out. It is this small figure who gives meaning to the whole scene. He is Cosmos, the hungry world waiting to be nourished by the Word of God and by the Body of Christ. The apostles receive the Holy Spirit not for themselves, but for the world which waits for salvation. Everything we do in trying to build up the life of the Church has to be driven by that awareness of a world which waits, a world hungry for God, hungry for the good news.

Being a vibrant parish is not an end in itself. There is no Tidy Towns Competition for parishes. We need to be the best we can, not for our own satisfaction, but for the sake of other people, *'so that the world may believe'*. There is a wonderful little paragraph in Pope John Paul's encyclical *Familiaris Consortio*. It is in section 43 and it describes the essential Christian attitude, not just for the family, but for the Church and for all our relationships. The phrase used is *'disinterested availability'* – not that we should be uninterested, but that we should not relate to other people out of self-interest. We are meant to risk our own interest for the sake of others. That service of others is at the heart of all our pastoral development, both in building up relationships within the local Church community and in reaching out to others wherever we find them. It is beautifully symbolised in the liturgy of Holy

Week and Easter by the washing of the feet, the symbolic act used by Jesus himself at the Last Supper (Jn 13).

One thing we seem to forget in recent years is that we have to put this attitude of service into effect **consciously**. We have to do it on purpose. It is never easy, and the world around us tries to lower our morale by suggesting that to do good on purpose is somehow hypocritical, as if good actions could only be respected when they are either unconscious or we feel so good about doing them that they come easy. In fact, it takes real goodness to do the positive thing when you don't feel like it. Planning to do good is an essential part of moral development, whether for an individual or for a community, and we need the conscious support of each other if we are to progress as a faith community and a community of service.

## 2. STRATEGIC PLANNING

*'If you do not know where you are going,*
*you are sure to end up somewhere else' (Mark Twain)*

*'Jesus said to the servants: "Fill the jars with water", and they filled them to the brim.'*

When those involved in parish leadership embark on a process of parish development and renewal, it is vital that they trust in the process upon which they are embarking. In other words, if they believe in the value of what they are doing, it is essential that they trust in the power of the Holy Spirit to guide the process and bring it to fruition.

It is also essential that they use the tools that God puts at their disposal for the task: the ordinary human resources and skills which are relevant to what they wish to achieve. Since they will be dealing with a parish community, and individuals and groups within that community, they should look to people and processes which relate to communication and interaction within groups. Since they are also specifically addressing the development of this parish community into the future ('going forward', as the business people say), they will find the skills and processes of strategic planning particularly relevant. Business and community consultants who deal with strategic planning tend to have their own jargon and slogans, but they often express a truth which demands our attention. 'To fail to plan is to plan to fail' is an obvious example. Just because it is a truism doesn't mean it isn't true. It is as true for a parish as it is for a small business or for any local community initiative.

We have choices of course; we can be like the cork tossed around by the tide without direction and control or we can be like the ship, battling against the same tide but with a course set and a compass and tiller to help steer that course. In other words, we drift or we take control.

**Planning can bring considerable benefits:**

● It is an opportunity to take stock of where we are;

● It can help get things done and usually with better use of what are often scarce resources;

● It can give a focus to our efforts;

● It makes it easier for us to communicate what we do;

● It reduces the risk of mistakes or surprises;

● It provides opportunities for people to become involved;

● It allows us to monitor progress.

A planning process within a parish brings the added benefits of revitalising parishes, re-kindling enthusiasm and renewing hope.

As in every aspect of life there are those who will be in favour of a planning process and those who are not convinced of its value; in fact some people will try to block a planning process, often using the reason that a plan will only raise expectations which cannot be fulfilled. These are spurious arguments and do not do justice to our people. People are not fools and have a very realistic understanding of what is possible. The question can also be asked: what is wrong with raising expectations? There are many examples in Ireland today of developments which would never have happened if people of vision and energy had not raised expectations. Very often today, people need to have their expectations raised. For many reasons people have almost learnt not to have expectations; don't look for something and then if you don't get it you won't be disappointed. What a negative attitude to life. Are we not the people of hope?

There are of course, all types of plans: business plans, financial plans and development plans, to name but a few. Strategic planning is a process which is used extensively by organisations to plot a course of action for the future. The process asks some very basic questions:

- What is happening within our organisation and what is happening outside our organisation which might impact on what we want to do?

- What are the strengths and weaknesses within our organisation?

- What are the opportunities and threats we may face?

- What changes do we want to effect? In other words, what is our vision for the future?

- What is our mission, why do we exist, what is our purpose?

- What aims or goals might we set ourselves as we try to achieve our vision?

- What tasks need to be accomplished if we are to realise those aims or goals?

- What targets can we set so we will know we have achieved our aims or goals?

- What resources will we need to enable us to carry out the tasks we have set for ourselves? Where and how might we access these resources?

- When will we carry out our tasks? What is our programme of work?

- How will we monitor and evaluate our progress?

This is a long list of questions and so straightaway it needs to be recognised that producing a parish strategic plan is not a quick fix. From start to finish it could take between one and two years to produce a plan. However, remember the Chinese bamboo seed; if you plant it and water it nothing will appear above ground for four years but in the fifth year the seed will sprout up to 80 feet and all because it has been tended for four years. Remember also the law of the farm; it is not possible to reap what you have not sown and if the seeds are not tended or watered there will be a very poor crop. Embarking on a strategic planning process within a parish will need time; time to gather a group to manage the process, time to train and develop that group, time to consult parishioners, time to discuss the outcome from the consultation and time to develop the response to the feedback.

The strategic planning process makes new demands on all involved. It is unfamiliar territory for both priest and people: they have not been trained for this process and may understandably be nervous. That is one reason for starting the process with a special novena or mission or time of prayer in the parish. Another reason, of course, is to ask God's blessing on the work and yet another is to prepare people for the process.

This chapter suggests a structured approach to strategic planning at parish level which has been tried and tested in a number of parishes, including Ardmore.

**Step one: decide on who will do the work**

There are a number of options; some parishes have established pastoral councils or core groups and tasked these groups with the preparation of the plan, often with some external help. Other parishes have gone for external help to lead a parish planning process from which a pastoral council or core group emerges and then takes on responsibility for the implementation of the plan.

Local circumstances will often influence the final decision but our preference would be for a group to be established at an early stage – this can be a steering group until the planning process itself is complete – and that this group has access to some external expertise from the beginning of the process. This approach can help engender the maximum ownership of the process.

Whatever option is chosen it is essential that the whole parish is fully aware of what is happening and why. It is particularly essential that existing parish organisations are kept fully informed as sometimes there can be the perception that a new group is taking over and they will no longer be required. Of course, the opposite is the truth. The key task of any core group or pastoral council in this process is to maximise the contributions of others.

**Step two: examine where we are now**

Every planning process starts with an assessment of the current position. In the case of parishes this can be done in a variety of ways:

- Desk research; this entails firstly consulting parish records as from these we can see trends, for example, in numbers being baptised, numbers dying, numbers marrying and so on. We can consult statutory sources of information such as the census returns. (In the Republic, www.cso.ie and in Northern Ireland www.nisra.gov.org)

- Meeting with and listening to parish organisations; one spin-off output from the process can be a directory of parish organisations, especially in long established parishes where many organisations are taken for granted and newcomers may never actually find out about them.

- Holding special listening exercises open to everyone in the parish; included in this might be special events for young people. These could be focus groups to which small numbers of people are invited and which are facilitated by someone who ideally has experience in leading small groups. There is usually a set agenda and someone apart from the facilitator records the discussion.

- Inviting direct feedback to the parish office or to the parish website if one exists.

- Designing and distributing a special questionnaire for completion at all Masses on a particular weekend. **A sample questionnaire is included in Section E: Resource Materials,** but a word of advice; questionnaire design is a specialist task so it can be worth getting professional help. The questions you ask determine the answers and hence the feedback you will get. Remember also that the completed questionnaires need to be analysed; not such an issue if you only have a few dozen but when you have hundreds or more it is quite a piece of work. Questionnaire analysis is a specialist process as dedicated computer programmes are used to carry out the work efficiently and to enable the data to be presented in a way we can all understand.

● Have the core group/pastoral council undertake a Strengths/ Weaknesses/ Opportunities/Threats analysis of the parish. Remember that Strengths and Weaknesses are internal:, they are within the parish itself. Opportunities and Threats are generally outside the parish. An example is set out below of some of the things which might emerge from such an exercise:

| STRENGTHS | WEAKNESSES |
|---|---|
| Pro-active parish clergy<br>Good range of<br>parish organisations<br>Modernised parish hall<br>Good school | Lack of volunteers<br>in many organisations<br>Declining church attendances<br>Declining parish collections |
| OPPORTUNITIES | THREATS |
| Make more use<br>of the parish hall<br>Develop special liturgies<br>for young people<br>Build ecumenical linkages<br>Celebrate good marriages | Loss of curate<br>Continuing failure<br>to attract volunteers<br>Continuing scandals<br>in the church |

● Again with the core group/pastoral council discuss the needs the parish could or should be meeting and the things which are driving the parish forward or holding it back.

In an ideal world all of the above should be used but resources may put constraints on the scope of the consultation. Our advice is to do the most widespread consultation you can. It is absolutely critical that any plan which emerges from this process is owned by the parishioners; if it is seen as the parish priest's plan or the core group/pastoral council's plan, people will be much more reluctant to invest in its implementation.

Whichever process you use, the end result should be a report which summarises all the findings and sets out any assumptions you think should guide the development of any plan. For example, you might assume:

● Numerically, the parish will grow but numbers practising their religion will continue to decline

● The parish is likely to lose a curate within the next two years given the shortage of priests within the diocese

● Parish organisations will continue to find it difficult to recruit and retain volunteers

● Marriage break-ups will increase

● Co-habiting will increase

● Drug and alcohol dependencies will increase

● Many young people may not practise but will want to be challenged spiritually and to be active socially and so on.

This report then needs to be brought to the attention of the parishioners. Again, there are a variety of ways of doing this but we consider that all of these should be done. A leaflet should be produced and sent to every household in the parish; members of the core group/pastoral council should present the report at Masses over a weekend; there should be a special Parish Assembly at which the report should be presented and discussed. **A draft agenda for a Parish Assembly is included in Section E: Resources.**

**Step three: prepare your vision for the parish**

This is in many ways one of the most critical steps in the process. Vision is the most powerful tool which motivates and energises people, especially if they understand and own the vision and have had an opportunity to contribute to it. Forming the vision should be an integral part of the work of the Parish Assembly. Parishioners should have the chance, having heard of the issues, to indicate the kind of parish they want in 5 or 10 years time. The ideas can be grouped under various headings to be worked on after the Assembly. Ideas for development can also be found in official Church sources.

Here are six key areas following the themes of Vatican II and official Church teaching since then. (In Ardmore, we introduced these by a Scripture reflection on the Marriage Feast of Cana. We saw each area as a water jar which we could fill to the brim.)

- Building community

- Ecumenism

- Social issues

- Empowerment of the laity

- Involvement of children and young people

- Marriage and family life

Taking each of these areas for development, ask people to say what changes they would like to see. This process will result in many ideas, some of which will be more useful and practical than others, but the core group/pastoral council will need to take all the ideas and consider them in depth after the Assembly.

Step four: decide your purpose or mission

At a meeting after the Assembly the core group/pastoral council needs to think about the suggestions which were made, and agree the parish Mission Statement. The Mission Statement should be as concise as possible and should pass the elevator test: you are delivering an application for funding for your organisation to a major Government Body and you are in the lift on your own going up five floors to deliver the application. Just as the doors are about to close the Chief Executive of the Department comes into the lift to join you; you have about one minute to tell him/her what your organisation does and why. A Mission Statement can and should be brief, e.g. 'The Catholic parish of Newry is a Christian faith community which is based on our love for God and for all our people and which is committed to serve all in our parish'.

Step five: decide the aims or goals you want to pursue

This is primarily a task for the core group/pastoral council. Taking each 'water jar' theme and considering the ideas which emerged from the vision-building process at the Parish Assembly, the group needs to decide what are the objectives we can set for ourselves under each theme. An example is given below:

**Marriage and Family Life:**

**Objective:** celebrate the marriages we have in our parish

**Objective:** prepare our young people for marriage

**Objective:** support families, including lone parents, in difficulties

Step six: agree the tasks which need to be undertaken for each objective

Again, this is a task for the core group/pastoral council. Taking each objective in turn the group agrees the actions needed to achieve the objective. An example is given below:

**Objective:** celebrate marriage

**Task:** Hold special Masses each year for those celebrating 25 years, 50 years of marriage that year; present each couple with a small gift from the parish

**Task:** Have a special liturgy on a day such as the Feast of the Holy Family; make part of this an opportunity for couples to renew their marriage vows

**Task:** Hold a parish dance or social function for married couples
This exercise is repeated for each objective.

Step seven: set targets

Again, this is a task for the core group/pastoral council. Taking each task in turn the group agrees the numbers and timescale. An example is given below:

**Task:** hold a special liturgy on the Feast of the Holy Family

**Target:** 30 families attending, begin preparations in October each year, hold event at end of December

**Step eight: identify resources**

Again, this is a task for the core group/pastoral council. Taking each task in turn the group agrees who will be responsible for implementation, how much the action will cost, if anything, and where the money will come from. An example is given below:

**Task:** hold a special liturgy on the feast of the Holy Family

**Resources:** the liturgy will be organised by the parish Liturgy Group (or ACCORD or Marriage Encounter, Teams of Our Lady etc) Costs will be special leaflets and tea/coffee afterwards in the parish centre; total estimate £100. Costs will be met from parish resources.

**Step nine: prepare the draft plan**

All of this detail is then assembled into a parish plan. A page, or more if necessary, should be produced for each theme along the lines set out below:

**Theme:** Marriage and Family Life

**Objective:** Celebrate Marriage

| TASKS | TARGETS | TIMESCALE | COSTS | IMPLEMENTATION |
|---|---|---|---|---|
| 1. Special Masses for anniversaries | | | | |
| 2. Liturgy on Feast of Holy Family | 30 families attending | Start October for celebration in late December | £100 | Parish Liturgy Group |
| 3. Social function | | | | |

**Objective:** Prepare young people for marriage

| TASKS | TARGETS | TIMESCALE | COSTS | IMPLEMENTATION |
|---|---|---|---|---|
| 1. | | | | |

**Objective:** support families, including lone parents, in difficulties

| TASKS | TARGETS | TIMESCALE | COSTS | IMPLEMENTATION |
|---|---|---|---|---|
| 1. | | | | |

### Step ten: submit the plan for approval to the parish

This should be done at a second Parish Assembly but copies of the plan should also be sent to every home and members of the core group/pastoral council should present the plan at Masses over a weekend. A month should be allowed for people to submit comments and then the plan should be formally adopted, perhaps at a special Mass or liturgy.

### Implementation:

*The process of working together is actualy more important than what we achieve.*

Preparing the plan is in many ways only the beginning; the plan has to be implemented. Be prepared for 'implementation dip' as people who have been working very hard and think their job is done realise the work is only starting. Putting the plan into action requires careful management. People can often be put off by the apparent scale of the task and so it is important to remind them that we do not have to complete the plan in a year or two. There is no real rush. The process of working together is actually more important than what we achieve. Break down the work into small chunks and involve as many people as possible in the process. There can be sense in setting up sub-groups for each of the themes; these should be led by members of the core group/pastoral council, but should have members with special interests or expertise also. Pay particular attention to the involvement of existing parish organisations and make sure they are included. Give the sub-groups the power and resources to do the work and trust them to get on with it but remember that

responsibility cannot be delegated and should stay with the core group/pastoral council. Reporting back arrangements should be in place but should be simple.

Arrange to meet annually and review progress; such a meeting could be attended by the core group/pastoral council and all the members of the sub-groups.

Remember also the need to continue developing and supporting the members of the groups; it is critical to keep sharpening the saw.

### 3. SUMMARY OF PROCESS

The process described here has been followed very closely in Newry, Co. Down, Ardmore, Derry, Inniskeen, Co. Monaghan and Tempo, Co. Fermanagh, but the elements of it have been found to be effective in the experience of the parish assemblies in Cork, and in Dublin parishes following the PDR programme, for example. The dynamic of people working together in parishes is pretty similar no matter where they are.

*"'Stand up," he said, "Do not be afraid." And when they raised their eyes they saw no-one but only Jesus.'*

### 1. Parish Mission

The process needs to begin with a motivational experience. A parish mission is very appropriate because it includes reflection and exhortation, and will be based on prayer and Scripture, which are vital to the dynamic of preparing a community to be led by the Spirit. If a mission is involved, the mission team needs to be briefed in advance: the mission should not emphasise a private spirituality, nor should there be an attitude of convening people for a week of mission only to dismiss them at the end of the week 'back to normal life'. This mission is going to be the beginning of something that will last. A parish festival or fun-day on the final Sunday of the mission can emphasise that the mission is not over, and can celebrate the reality of family and parish community.

### 2. Listening Exercise

As part of the exploration of the present reality of the parish, a questionnaire circulated at Masses on the last weekend of the parish mission can gather a wide cross-section of views, and can further emphasise that the end of the mission is really the beginning of a new phase in the life of the parish. When the responses to the questionnaire have been professionally analysed, a report, or a summary of the report, can be circulated to every home in the parish, with an invitation to attend a Parish Assembly.

### 3. Parish Assembly

The Parish Assembly is primarily an opportunity for parishioners to meet. It needs to be several hours long, possibly part of Saturday and Sunday afternoon. The extended time will allow parishioners to develop a vision for the parish, produce a draft mission statement and select a number of areas as priorities for development.

The process of the parish assembly should include prayer, Scripture and group interaction (discussion and sharing). An outside facilitator or facilitators can make a huge difference. People respond well when they feel that they are being genuinely listened to.

### 4. Carrying the Process Forward

As the Parish Assembly moves towards a conclusion, it will be evident that many good ideas will be lost unless some structure is put in place to carry them forward. Those present can delegate a few people to act as a working group on a short-term basis.

Rather than carrying things forward indefinitely themselves, this group's main purpose will be to arrange for the setting up of a Parish Pastoral Council. The Parish Pastoral Council will then work with the Parish Priest and other parish staff to pursue the ideas and projects from the Parish Assembly, and to guide the pastoral development of the parish.

### 5. Parish Pastoral Council

The Parish Pastoral Council will usually consist of ex officio members (parish priest, curate, parish sister or other full-time parish staff), elected members (from geographical areas or other constituencies), and co-opted members (usually to ensure gender balance, age balance etc.). As soon as a Pastoral Council is established, there is need for an induction and formation process for all the members. The parish priest should also participate in the training along with the other members, and an experienced facilitator is essential. Formation and training should continue for a number of months before any major projects are undertaken.

After a few months' experience of working together, members should elect a chairperson and a communications secretary. If there is a parish secretary in place, she/he might act as a non-voting member of the Pastoral Council and record the minutes. A draft constitution, for eventual approval by the bishop, should address issues like number of members, term of office, and a cycle of renewal of membership (for example, three or four years, with a number of members retiring each year and being replaced). **A sample Draft Constitution is included in Section E: Resources.**

### 6. Prayer, Scripture and Decision-making

The collaborative approach to parish leadership involves meeting, spending time together and together addressing what is important for us as a local faith community in this parish. The Greek word which underlies the word 'Church' in the New Testament is *'ekklesia'*, in Latin *'ecclesia'*, which became *'église'* in French and *'eaglais'* in Irish. It comes from the Greek verb *'to call'*. As Church we are a people called together.

*Prayer, Scripture and the guidance of the Holy Spirit.*

The whole parish community is called together as the pilgrim people of God and as the Body of Christ. This is expressed particularly as we gather for the Eucharist. The Parish Pastoral Council is called together as a more intense expression of the parish faith community. The meetings of the Parish Pastoral Council are not just business meetings. They should be marked by prayer and Scripture and openness to the guidance of the Holy Spirit. The process of decision making has to reflect this faith dimension. Secular decision-making, in business or politics, is often a battle of wills, an adversarial process ultimately resolved by a vote. In a Parish Pastoral Council the process is not my will against yours, but each of us prayerfully seeking the will of God, guided by the Holy Spirit. However, it is important to remember that we are not used to this kind of consensus decision making. The world has been training us all our lives through secular values. It will take a lot of time and practice to develop the processes of ecclesial leadership. What we are learning is in contrast to the world's ways.

It is also, if the truth be told, in contrast with how we have become accustomed to work in our Church organisations, including the running of our parishes and our dioceses. If we are to achieve the necessary levels of change and development, it will require significant investment of time and money. It will require a serious commitment to training. Priests will have to go through the training processes along with their people, as they learn to work together, to pray together, to progress together.

The cost of training may be reduced if a number of parishes group together to bring training opportunities to their locality. Conferences like the Developing Parish conference in All Hallows College, Dublin, and conferences run by the National Conference of Priests, can provide speakers and facilities which would not usually be available locally. These conferences also create a context for networking: people in one place can derive great encouragement and insight from people engaged in the same process in other places.

The Dublin Handbook for Parish Pastoral Councils has substantial material for training. Groups like the **Love is for Life Trust** (*www.loveisforlife.com*) and the **Armagh Office of Pastoral Renewal and Family Ministry** (*www.parishandfamilylife.ie*) can provide training and facilitation. Individuals like Martin Kennedy (Boora Co. Offaly) bring a wide range of experience and skills to respond to a growing need.

The training which is needed is not a formal academic training in the first instance. Those who become involved in parish pastoral councils need skills training and experience in working in a group process and a partnership model. Relevant skills would include: committee skills; group working; facilitation; communication, including writing, speaking, listening; planning skills; organisational skills; administration; vision building; negotiating; conflict resolution; and networking skills.

It will be of huge benefit to parishes if training and support is provided at diocesan level. We already have a model in the archdiocese of Dublin. The archdiocese not only has a diocesan pastoral resource office, but has also made provision within each parish pastoral council for a diocesan contact person whose role is to keep in touch with the diocesan office.

## 4. CALLING THE COMMUNITY

Renewal and development of a parish has to be rooted in the reality of the faith community. St Paul, writing to Timothy (2 Tim 1:6) said 'Fan into a flame the gift of God that you possess through the laying on of my hands'. Though addressed originally to one person, it applies also to the faith community of the parish, called to renew its commitment to Christ and his Church, and to bring energy and vitality to the living of the Christian life.

The parish community meets on a regular basis. Parishioners gather for Sunday Mass, for weekday Mass, and for sacramental and other celebrations, most notably at Christmas and during Holy Week and Easter. But when a process of renewal and development is being initiated, we need an extraordinary convocation: a calling together of the parish community specifically to stir up faith.

One of the obvious ways of stirring up that faith is the Parish Mission. The Parish Mission is traditional. It is well established and respected, and has overtones of continuity with the faith of past generations. Yet it is still a live and relevant experience, and in many parishes has the capacity to draw large numbers of people, young and old.

The Parish Mission should not be seen, however, as an isolated event. In the context of renewal and development of a parish community, it has to be the beginning of a process which can be sustained. For that reason, it is not enough to contact a Mission team or individual Mission leader and invite them to come and 'give a Mission' based on their own inspiration of the moment. The individual leader or team needs to be carefully chosen for their sensitivity to the realities of parish life, and for their willingness to plan a Mission in the light of the pastoral situation of the parish at this time. The planning of the Mission should be a collaborative exercise. It is not a convene-dismiss event whose meaning and relevance are self contained. It is designed to flow from the parish community and to call the parish community into a new phase of its life, into a new stage of its journey in faith.

## Preparation for the Mission

*'I pray for them. I am not praying for the world, but for those you have given me, because they belong to you. May they all be one.'*

As well as the collaborative planning with the Mission leader or team, the preparation within the parish is vital. If the Mission is planned for May or June, Holy Week is a good starting point for preparing the parish, since Holy Week and the Easter Triduum are themselves a celebration of Church, of being an Easter people in whom the presence of the Risen Christ is alive and active. The lead up to Pentecost is a good opportunity to emphasise that we are a people led by the Spirit, and anxious to discern where the Spirit is leading us as a faith community. If the Mission takes place at a different time of year, an effort should be made to link the preparation with the liturgy of the time. This period of preparation should be a period of prayer. Many parishes find that a special parish prayer leading up to the Mission can help to focus people's minds. It can be printed on a prayer card for use at home and in the Church, and could, for example, be used to conclude the Prayer of the Faithful at all Masses during these weeks. **A sample Parish Prayer is included in Section E: Resources.**

If a Pastoral Council already exists in the parish, or a core group or planning group of any kind, they can make a huge contribution to the planning of the Mission, meeting and interacting with the priests and Mission leadership team, articulating the needs and strengths of the parish, and bringing their experience to bear on the practicalities of the Mission timetable and the details of arrangements. **A sample Mission Plan is included in Section E: Resources.**

On the final week of the Mission, in the Masses of Saturday night and Sunday morning, the emphasis is on continuity: the Mission is not over. It is only beginning. That is symbolised by the Questionnaire on parish life which will be filled in after the Gospel of each Mass, in preparation for a process of parish development. Another symbol is the invitation to parishioners, young and old, to gather for a Parish Festival Day to celebrate the Mission and the ongoing life of the Parish.

In any community it is difficult to know what most people are thinking, what they want, what they are willing to contribute. This is particularly true of a community like a parish which is so big, so diverse, so complicated. Attempts are made at times to consult by putting on meetings. Few enough people turn up to those and even among those who do the majority don't say anything. The conclusion then is reached that it is impossible. And so the drift continues and the energy level of the Church remains low.

*'Every time we are with one another, we make Christ present through our company with one another and we meet him there.'*

## Parish Questionnaire

In this process, the Parish Questionnaire is a very effective means of consulting the parish community. It should come at the end of the Parish Mission Week when very many of the people are enthused with the great possibilities our faith holds for ourselves and our world. The weekend Masses are the ideal opportunity for this. Those giving the Mission Week should have been preparing the people for this Questionnaire both indirectly through their preaching and also directly by mentioning it throughout the week as what this special week is leading up to. The Questionnaire can then be presented to the people at the weekend Masses by those who have been leading the Mission. It is placed at the time of the Homily and should not take more time to do than the Homily would normally take. Those presenting it at each Mass can easily talk people through it, encouraging them to fill it in section by section. It is a very important and solemn occasion because it is, for very many, the first time their voice will be heard on how they see the parish and how they would like to see the parish in the years ahead.

## Need for Professionals

A questionnaire, if it is to be helpful, needs to be set up properly. It is not just a matter of asking the right questions, but of putting questions and the response to questions in a form that will permit analysis in a systematic way, preferably by computer. It is wise to take professional advice beforehand, and if possible to have the analysis afterwards carried out by professionals who will be able to make the most of the information and present it in an accessible form. **A sample Questionnaire is included in Section E: Resources.**

**For Everyone?**

Not everybody who will be present for the weekend Masses will have been at the Mission Week. They need to be acknowledged in how the Questionnaire is presented. And not everyone in the parish will be present for the weekend Masses. Some regular attenders may be away. Others who belong to the parish will have given up going to Mass. Those present should be asked to take copies of the Questionnaire home with them for those they know would not otherwise receive it. Copies can also be left in local shops or surgeries for a couple of weeks where people can pick them up and complete them. However, the reality is that few, if any, will fill in this Questionnaire other than those who do so at the weekend Masses. But that does not in any way invalidate the importance for the parish of what will come out of this Questionnaire.

**A Statement of Intent**

As has been said, attending to the Questionnaire in this way at the weekend Mass is a clear statement that the Mission is not ended but rather is only beginning in a new and different way. It also needs to be a statement of intent to take the answers to the Questionnaire seriously and to follow them all up in ways that are observable. In order to do this the filled in Questionnaires need to be analysed. There are firms who do this on a computer programme that produces a very clear picture of the parish through the eyes of the parishioners. We include one page of the results of the Questionnaire that was filled in during the weekend Masses in the parish of Ardmore, Derry. This gives an idea of what the whole resulting booklet looks like.

**Back to the Community**

Once the Questionnaire has been analysed, it is comparatively simple to have a booklet printed, giving at least a summary of the outcomes. A copy of this booklet should be delivered to every home in the parish. This is important because then everyone has the opportunity to see what the parish looks like through eyes other than their own. The strengths and weaknesses will all be there. The task of the parish then becomes to build up the strengths and address the weaknesses so that, working together, the parish can be a place where everyone is cared for and everyone has the opportunity to contribute. The next stage of the process, the Parish Assembly, has a very important part to play in this development.

**A sample of the results of the first seven questions from the questionnaire:**

**ST MARY'S ARDMORE PARISH SURVEY 2000**
**Relationships and Involvement in the Parish**

The Quality of Relationships between Priests and People is

| %         | %    | %    | %    | %          |     |
|-----------|------|------|------|------------|-----|
| Excellent | Good | Fair | Poor | Don't Know | N   |
| 54.6      | 54.6 | 6.5  | 1.3  | 2.0        | 540 |

Relationships between the People and the Schools are

| %         | %    | %    | %    | %          |     |
|-----------|------|------|------|------------|-----|
| Excellent | Good | Fair | Poor | Don't Know | N   |
| 23        | 39.2 | 18.2 | 2.6  | 16.9       | 538 |

The work of Parish Organisations is

| %         | %    | %    | %    | %          |     |
|-----------|------|------|------|------------|-----|
| Excellent | Good | Fair | Poor | Don't Know | N   |
| 28.5      | 43.7 | 16.2 | 1.9  | 9.7        | 536 |

Co-operation between Parish Organisations is

| %         | %    | %    | %    | %          |     |
|-----------|------|------|------|------------|-----|
| Excellent | Good | Fair | Poor | Don't Know | N   |
| 20.4      | 37.9 | 16.1 | 3.3  | 22.2       | 514 |

Involvement of Women in the Parish is

| %         | %    | %    | %    | %          |     |
|-----------|------|------|------|------------|-----|
| Excellent | Good | Fair | Poor | Don't Know | N   |
| 21.5      | 47.9 | 16.8 | 3.4  | 10.4       | 530 |

Involvement of Men in the Parish is

| %         | %    | %    | %    | %          |     |
|-----------|------|------|------|------------|-----|
| Excellent | Good | Fair | Poor | Don't Know | N   |
| 18.2      | 47   | 20.1 | 5    | 9.8        | 523 |

The Process of Decision Making is

| % Excellent | % Good | % Fair | % Poor | % Don't Know | N |
|---|---|---|---|---|---|
| 15.7 | 34.1 | 21.1 | 5.1 | 24.1 | 511 |

## 6. GATHERING THE COMMUNITY

A Parish Assembly, the next stage in this process, should be arranged for two or three months after the Mission Week. This is a short enough time to keep the momentum of all that has happened. It is a long enough time to have the Questionnaires analysed, the results distributed to the people of the parish, and to give everyone a chance to catch their breath! An invitation to the Parish Assembly should go to each home along with the booklet showing the results of the Questionnaire.

*'A primary task for us as followers of Christ is to build the Church as a people of joy and gladness.'*

### For Whom?

We recommend that the Parish Assembly be open to everyone over sixteen years of age because of the attention span that will be required for this event. Not everyone will come to it but everyone needs to know that they are invited and wanted. This will take a lot of advertising and promotion within the parish so that those who do come to it cannot in any way be seen as a clique and so are free to make decisions for the parish.

### Purpose

The purpose of the Parish Assembly is two-fold

1.  **To review the findings of the Questionnaire**

2.  **In the light of those findings, to begin the development of a pastoral plan for the parish.**

Because of this two-fold purpose a Parish Assembly has to be given a substantial amount of time. The temptation could be to try to do it in an evening in the hope that this might attract more people. Because of its importance to the future of the parish this temptation should be resisted!

## Proposed Schedule/Agenda

We suggest that the best approach to the Parish Assembly is to think of it as a Saturday and Sunday and facilitated by a competent person or team.

**Saturday:**

**11.00am:** Welcome, Introductions, Opening Prayer, Expectations, Guidelines

**11.20am:** **Where We Are Now?**
1. A presentation on the findings of the Questionnaire.

2. *Looking at our Survey, which are the three most important things that have emerged for you?*
A few minutes for each person to write answer.
Small group sharing on this
Full group sharing – using flipchart

**12.00pm:** *What kind of parish do we want?*
Working towards a vision statement for the parish

Having now established our vision for our parish, the question arises:
**How do we move towards its fulfilment?**

**Six Vital Building Blocks Are:**

**Building community with one another**

**Ecumenism:** building unity with other Christian Churches and other religions – not forgetting our own Catholic people who may be alienated from us.

**Social Issues of justice and peace and equality**

**Empowerment of the Laity**

**Involvement of Children and Young People**

**Marriage and Family Life:**
the Domestic Church

**For a fuller treatment of these cf. Part 2: the Wedding feast of Cana**

1.00pm:    Lunch

2.00pm:    Divide into six groups and give each group one of the six areas of living faith with the following questions:

*What are our goals or aims for moving forward?*

*For each goal or aim: what objectives do we have?*

*For each objective: what actions might we take?*

4.00pm:    Review of Day
           Agenda for Sunday
           Closing Prayer

**Sunday:**
The Parish Assembly should be part of the focus for the weekend Masses, assuring people that even if they were not present on Saturday they are very welcome for the Sunday part.

2.00pm:    Welcome, Opening Prayer, Recap Saturday

2.15pm:    *What resources do we have for moving forward in the ways indicated on Saturday?*

*What other resources will we need?*

*How and where will we get those resources?*

3.30pm:    Break

3.45pm:    *How will we organise ourselves to take this plan forward? Discussion should lead to options, the best of which is likely to be a Parish Pastoral Council.*

*How can we ensure we will bring the parish along with us?*

**5.00pm:** *Where do we go from here?*

Set up a working group of five or six people from among those present who will organise the election of the Pastoral Council within two months.

**5.30pm:** Review of Assembly/Closing Prayer

**See Section E: Resources
for Outcomes of Parish Assembly.**

## 7. EMPOWERED BY THE COMMUNITY

Once a decision has been made to establish a Parish Pastoral Council, there are basic steps which need to be taken to determine the membership.

*'Know that I am with you always, yes to the end of time.'*

● Most Pastoral Councils consist of ex officio members, elected members and co-opted members.

**Ex officio** members are those already appointed to leadership in the parish, most obviously the priest or priests. In some parishes these could include a religious, like a parish sister, and possibly a lay person in an appointed position like a pastoral co-ordinator.

**Co-opted members** are added to the number of ex officio and elected members, usually either to address gender or age balance, or because of special experience or expertise or recognised commitment. They are invited by the parish priest, but this should follow a process of consultation and discernment with the other members.

**Elected members** form a vital part of the parish pastoral council, yet it is this element which can give rise to the greatest degree of fear and hesitation. Some parish priests shy away from a pastoral council for this reason, and instead form a core group or other advisory committee made up of invited members only, who may remain in place for years almost unchanged. There is obvious good will here, in that the priest wants to have a collaborative approach and responsible advice from committed parishioners. But there is also fear. The fear that is often expressed is that the wrong people might be elected: people who by a negative or confrontational attitude might hold up any process of development rather than encourage it.

- Where pastoral councils exist, the very widespread experience is that rarely, if ever, does the election of members result in a negative outcome. Parishioners demonstrate a great deal of wisdom and discernment in choosing who they will elect to represent them. Once it is clear that this is a **pastoral** council, concerned with the spiritual and pastoral development of the whole parish, those who might seek political influence or power for themselves will no longer be interested, and parishioners will vote for genuinely committed people who have the parish at heart. At worst, a good person might be elected who could prove to be impatient with discussing the overview of pastoral development, and who would say, 'Tell me what needs to be done and let me get on with it'. Someone who prefers to work for the parish in a different way will resolve that sooner or later by taking on another role. But even that is rare.

When Jesus told his disciples so often: *'Do not be afraid'*, we should not assume that he was merely addressing personal phobias. It is at least as likely that, speaking to those who formed the nucleus of the early church, he was saying, *'Don't be afraid to take risks in your evangelisation or pastoral development'*. In relation to pastoral council elections, the gain in broadly based collaborative leadership is of such value that it more than offsets any risk that might be involved.

- Decisions have to be made about constituencies for elections, and about the electoral process to be used. Generally speaking, constituencies will be based on geographical areas in the parish. These often define themselves, as people will have a perception of their area, or areas will already exist for sick visitation etc. It is important not to multiply small areas, or the numbers on the pastoral council will become unwieldy. And it is important to leave room for co-opted members.

- The electoral process can be very simple. Some method of taking proposals (such as a form included in the parish newsletter) will give a number of names. The most frequently proposed names can then be included in a voting paper (for example, the top three names from each constituency), and the voting paper can be distributed at all Masses on a particular weekend. It only takes a few minutes after the Gospel for people to mark their choice (X or 1, 2, 3) on the voting paper, choosing a person from their own area of the parish. The voting papers are collected immediately and can be counted after Mass.

- Co-opted members need to be chosen carefully. The first thing to watch out for is that the process of co-opting members should be kept separate from the electoral process. There is an understandable temptation to co-opt all those who were next in line in the elections. But if all those next in line are co-opted in order of voting, the value of co-option to address age and gender balance and so on is lost. However, an individual should not necessarily be excluded just because they were nominated but not elected in the original voting.

- Co-opted members can be chosen to achieve an appropriate age balance or gender balance, or to bring someone on to the pastoral council who has a particular skill or experience or known commitment, for example a track record for dedicated voluntary work. The existing members, ex officio and elected, should make a list of possible members, giving reasons for suggesting them. The parish priest will then invite a number of these to join the pastoral council, taking account of the suggestions and the views of the existing members. The total number of members should neither be too small or too large, depending on the size of the parish. Twelve or fifteen should suffice for a small or medium sized parish. Anything over twenty is becoming less flexible even for a large parish. Not all members may be able to be present at every meeting, but regular attendance is vital. **Sample documents included in Section E: Resources.**

# 8. SEVEN HABITS OF HIGHLY EFFECTIVE PARTNERSHIPS

Partnership working is a relatively new and much misunderstood way of working.

A partnership at its simplest is at least two organisations or groupings of people acting together by contributing their diverse resources to pursue a common vision with clearly defined goals and objectives.

There are some key words in that short definition:

- **Acting together:** this does not mean that everyone does the same thing at the same time but rather that members of the partnership recognise the particular strengths which a member has and play to that strength. Everyone is fully aware of what is happening and why and what the expected results are and has agreed the actions and timescale. There is clarity around roles and responsibilities and contributions.

- **Contributing their diverse resources:** each partner brings different gifts to the table. In fact, if all brought the same gifts there could be little reason for collaboration. Some members bring particular skills or expertise, others bring local knowledge or contacts, some bring money or equipment or premises, some bring perceptions of what is possible. Members of the partnership do not have to contribute equally but they must contribute in proportion to their resources and abilities. A partnership could be put as 2+2 = 5. In other words it aims to deliver more than the sum of its constituent parts.

- **Pursue a common vision:** it is critical that partnerships invest as much time as they need to ensure that all members share the reasons for the partnership's existence and are fully aware of the desired outcomes. Again, not everyone may want the same outcomes; it is perfectly possible for a partnership to deliver different outcomes to different groups.

- **Clearly defined goals and objectives:** it is essential that the partnership is working to a plan which the members have agreed among themselves. This should set out the goals (the major steps) and objectives (the tasks needed to realise the goals) and identify who is responsible for implementation.

There is actually a hierarchy of partnership working:

- Co-operation
- Co-ordination
- Collaboration

The aim is to have a partnership where there is:

- **Leadership,** where the partners share a common vision and harness their energies and resources to achieve more than they could on their own

- **Trust,** where partners are mutually accountable to each other, share risks and rewards fairly and support each other; competition between members of a partnership is a sure sign of a failure of partnership working

- **Learning,** where the partners continuously seek to improve what they do in partnership

- **Managing for performance**, where the partners put in place the necessary practices and resources and manage change effectively.

If you can tick each of the following you have a healthy partnership:

| | |
|---|---|
| Partners can demonstrate **real results through collaboration** | |
| **Common interest** supersedes partner interest | |
| Partners use **'we'** when talking about partnership matters | |
| Partners are **mutually accountable** for tasks and outcomes | |
| Partners **share** responsibilities and rewards | |
| Partners strive to develop and maintain **trust** | |
| Partners are **willing to change** what they do and how they do it | |
| Partners **seek to improve** how the **partnership** performs | |

Partnership working can bring real benefits such as:

- Additional influence which one member on their own could not achieve
- A critical mass which justifies the use of resources and helps ensure results
- Shared resources leading to reduced individual costs for members
- Greater impact
- Added value to the work of individuals
- An opportunity to learn from others
- An opportunity to influence others
- The opportunity to be innovative; we are much more likely to be innovative when we can share the risks

However, we need to remember that some people can feel threatened by partnerships. They see them as interference or as extra work or as challenges to their particular way of working. If you have been accustomed to doing things your own way for a long time it is not so easy to change.

To help form and maintain good partnership working we set out below the Seven Habits of Highly Effective Partnerships (with acknowledgement to Stephen Covey, author of the *Seven Habits of Highly Effective People*).

### Habit One: Be proactive

This is the habit of taking personal responsibility; we have the ability to make a response to the situation we find ourselves in. We identify our circle of concern and then identify our circle of influence. In other words we are clear about the areas where we can make a difference; the rest we leave to others. Proactivity means adopting a positive approach and recognising that if it is to be it is up to me. 'They' will never do anything. If we are proactive we have certain values and these are the things which guide and drive us. Partnerships need to agree those values for themselves.

### Habit Two: Begin with the end in mind

This is the habit of developing and maintaining a focus on the vision for the partnership. In creating a vision for our parish we ask three questions. What are the things we want to keep? What are the things we want to change? What are the things we want to create? Answers to these help us build a vision of the parish and partnership we want. Beginning with the end in mind means measuring twice and cutting once. We take time to get it right.

### Habit Three: Put first things first

This is the habit of setting priorities. When we consult and listen to people a long list of needs and desires will appear. It is unlikely we will have the resources to tackle them all and so we can ask ourselves what is really important and then organise ourselves around those priorities. Another reason for setting priorities is the need for early achievements within partnership. Nothing builds success like success and there will be a need to show results as soon as possible.

### Habit Four: Think win/win

This is the habit of recognising that the best deals, the best agreements are those where everyone can feel they have gained something. They might not have got all they wanted but there is enough there for them to be able to say yes. Mutually beneficial agreements are the only real basis for building partnerships. Win/lose may work once but seldom twice. This habit asks us to believe in the abundance mentality rather than the scarcity mentality. If I believe everything is scarce I will not share, I will not collaborate. On the other hand, if I believe there is plenty out there and we can make more then I will be happy to share and work with others.

### Habit Five: Seek first to understand and then to be understood

This attitude, which we recognise from the prayer of St. Francis, is the habit of effective listening. We need to come to the partnership prepared to see the world as others see it and to listen at least as much as we talk. It means diagnosing the problem before we prescribe the solution.

### Habit Six: Synergize

This is the habit of strategic alliances and recognising that 2+2 makes 5. This is about networking, forming alliances to ensure issues can be addressed using the combined resources and expertise of all the members.

### Habit Seven: Sharpen the saw

This is the habit of renewal. We cannot expect partnerships just to go on forever; members need to take time out to re-charge the batteries. This can be one or more of the following: spiritual renewal, mental renewal, social renewal, physical renewal. It is essential to build in ongoing and regular time for renewal of their partnership. This can be periods of shared prayer or scripture study, training in new skills, a meal together, a walk. All of these things help in creating relationships and renewing commitments.

## 9. PARTNERSHIP
## WITH THE PASTORAL COUNCIL

### Introduction

*'We are prophets of a future not our own.'*

Through Baptism, Confirmation, Eucharist – the Sacraments of Christian Initiation – every individual Catholic is given the assurance of being cared for by the community of the Church.

Through these Sacraments also, each individual Catholic is given the right and responsibility to minister within the Church and to take part in the mission of the Church to evangelise the world we live in. In this chapter we look at a way of trying to fulfil the first of these, namely how we can keep that promise to care for every person baptised among us. In the next chapter, we will look at how we can call each person to live out their Christian right and responsibility to minister and evangelise.

### Forming a Pastoral Council

The Priest, appointed by the Bishop to the parish, has the primary responsibility for the pastoral care of all the parishioners. Clearly he cannot fulfil this alone, either from a practical point of view or from a proper understanding of the role of every parishioner who is baptised, confirmed, and shares in the priesthood of Christ. Gathering together a Pastoral

Council from among the parishioners would seem the best and most viable way to move forward in taking on this responsibility.

Here are a few important points about Pastoral Councils.

1.  The purpose of a Pastoral Council is the pastoral care of all the parishioners. Many of the pastoral needs of the people will have shown up in the questionnaire.

    Some of the ways of dealing with these needs will have surfaced in the work of the Parish Assembly. So these are the two basic documents for the development of the Pastoral Council.

2.  A Pastoral Council establishes partnership with the Parish Priest and others who may have been appointed to the pastoral care of the parishioners. The Parish Priest is the President of the Pastoral Council; other appointed people are ex officio members of it. Parishioners are part of it either through election by the parishioners or through co-option by the Parish Priest.

3.  A Pastoral Council is founded on partnership, and rooted firmly in the Scriptures, the traditions and teaching of the Catholic Church and is intent on listening to the call of God's Spirit in the world in which we live. There are City Councils, Urban Councils, County Councils and so on, whose origin and shape may look somewhat similar to what we are describing here. But there is a fundamental difference in that we are and must be engaged with the will of God, the way of God, the kingdom of God. St Paul wrote in one of his letters: *'Never say or do anything except in the name of the Lord Jesus, giving thanks to God the Father through him'* (Col 3, 17). That could be a wonderful description of what the spirit of a Pastoral Council should be.

### What is Partnership?

Attempts to establish Pastoral Councils often fail because of the human condition. Sometimes they fail because a particular Parish Priest insists on complete control and the ultimate right to make all decisions. In other circumstances they fail because of the laity trying to run things with as little reference as possible to the Parish Priest or the others who are in the parish by appointment. Power struggles are part and parcel of the human condition when any group of people is gathered together. Pastoral Councils are no exception! Developing a true sense of partnership is the way to steer clear of these power struggles or of getting back out of them when they occur. Some important points about partnership are:

1. Partnership has to be based on equality among the members of the Pastoral Council. This means developing equality of voice, of responsibility, of esteem. Sometimes people can look for equality of voice while not being willing to take on full responsibility and of course then it becomes unbalanced. Equally unbalanced is the situation where equality of responsibility is expected but an equal say is denied. In a situation like a Pastoral Council equality of esteem also gets severely tested as people can easily esteem others because of what they have in terms of wealth or education or social standing rather than by who they are as gifted by God.

2. Equality does not mean being the same. Consequently forming partnership as a Pastoral Council demands recognising and acknowledging the differences that exist in terms of role and of possibility. For example, the Parish Priest continues to have the ultimate responsibility for the pastoral care of the people of the parish. Forming partnership does not take this away. However, it does mean that this ultimate responsibility does not get in the way of him sharing his position fully with the others. Nor should it become some kind of excuse to leave everything to him. Ultimate responsibility means just that – the last point which may never need to be reached.

3. Being part of a Pastoral Council does not mean being put 'in charge' of the parish. It is easy for members of a Pastoral Council to fall into the trap of seeing themselves 'in charge' and consequently either burdened down by it or making it their possession and their little kingdom. Pastoral Council membership does mean being placed in a position of joint leadership in the parish. It's about learning to do leadership together. And it has to be a leadership towards helping every parishioner to take her or his rightful place in the community of the parish. The way of life of a Pastoral Council has to be

that of consensus leadership in which individuals are not going off simply on their own but are exercising their individual leadership in a spirit of true partnership with everyone else. Because of this, attendance at the monthly meetings is so vital. Because of this also it is important to have good communication going between the members in between meetings. And because of this it is imperative that the parish community is kept fully informed of what is on the various agendas of the Pastoral Council meetings and everything that is happening as a result.

Only experience will clarify what is meant by terms like empowerment and partnership. There is a great need for common sense and balance as everyone progresses through what can be a steep learning curve. It is not a case of power passing from the parish priest to a new power elite in the parish. The delegation of responsibility involves the delegation of accountability as well. There has to be a realism about what is involved. The parish priest cannot share control over the basic doctrines of the Church or over the Ten Commandments, because it is not his to share. But he can collaborate in a genuine way in finding the best way ahead for the pastoral life of the parish. And the more that sharing and collaboration becomes the norm both for the parish priest and for those who participate in responsibility, the more vibrant the life of the parish will be.

### Induction, Formation and Training

Before becoming active within the Community as a Pastoral Council the members should have an induction period for at least 3-6 months. This time is for their own formation as a group and also as individuals around the question of what we mean by pastoral care.

### Prayer & Scripture

Both prayer and Scripture are vital tools for discovering what pastoral care means. Through prayer we learn to see people through the eyes of God. God sees only the beauty and goodness of every person. Everyone is precious in God's eyes. When we depend on our own eyes we make distinctions and act accordingly. God also sees the wonderful potential in every person. With our eyes we at best mostly see their needs.

Through Scripture we also learn to see through the eyes of God and we are introduced into the huge world of God's creation and God's longing for everyone to know how much they are loved. We generally tend to live in the small world of our own self-importance or our self-preoccupations. The human person cannot live in a world without mountains. When we live in a small world mole hills will do and our energy is spent in climbing those mole hills. This can easily happen in a group like a Pastoral Council where the small world of self-importance or self-preoccupations blocks them from developing true pastoral care in the parish.

## Training

*Ongoing training is a necessity.*

These first few months of induction will bring to the surface the ways that the Pastoral Council will need training if they are going to be effective. Some of that training may even begin during this time but will by no means be completed. Ongoing training is a necessity. The training needs will include:

- The full meaning of being a Pastoral Council

- how best to conduct their meetings

- leadership and how best to conduct meetings with others

- The various roles within the Pastoral Council e.g. Chairperson, Assistant Chairperson; Communications Secretary, Assistant Communications Secretary (ref p. 87)

- reporting back to the community

- on-going listening to the community

- prayer

- Scripture

- tradition and teaching of the Church

- Eucharist

- evangelisation

## Where to Start?

1.  Within two weeks of the election of the Parish Pastoral Council the parish priest should convene a meeting of all those who have accepted their election. As well as this being an opportunity to meet one another, the main purpose of this meeting is to consult them about who should be co-opted as members of the Council. The things to keep in mind are gender and age balance and also who might have special gifts to bring to the group. The parish priest then takes the names of people that have been mentioned and asks each one personally until the required number is reached.

2.  Within two weeks of this meeting, another meeting of the full Pastoral Council is held. The purpose of this meeting is to get to know one another. At this meeting also the dates and places of the meetings of the Pastoral Council are established and agreed on so that everyone is able to be present for all the meetings and activities of the Council. This commitment to the Pastoral Council's meetings has to be seen as a real priority in the service that each one gives to the parish.

3.  Within the next month a full day – Saturday or Sunday – is held to begin the orientation of the Pastoral Council members to the full meaning and possibilities of what they have taken on. This day should be conducted by a trained facilitator or facilitating team, preferably those who facilitated the Parish Assembly. Obviously this day would need to have been arranged with the facilitator much earlier with two or three possible dates to choose from so that everyone can be accommodated. **Outline Formation Programme included in Section E: Resources.**

4.  The week after this day together the Pastoral council members are presented to the parish community and are commissioned for their new role at one of the significant Masses of the weekend. This is to let the Community know who the Council members both elected and co-opted are and to remind the Council members that their task is the service of this community.

5.  A series of six meetings, one per month, now begins: to continue and deepen the knowledge and commitment of the Council members and also to prepare them for action within

the Community These six meetings should also be conducted preferably by the facilitator/s who were at the Assembly and full day with the Pastoral Council. **Outline included in Section E: Resources.**

# 10. PARTNERSHIP
# THROUGH THE PASTORAL COUNCIL

## Introduction

The dynamic of pastoral development through collaborative ministry and the parish pastoral council is one which begins from the community and flows back to the community in a continuous cycle. The cycle has to be established and promoted consciously, because the natural inertia of human nature and parish life will tend to slow it down or even bring it to a stop.

*'May the message of Christ in all its richness find a home with you.'*
*(Col 3:16)*

The first phase of the cycle is setting up the pastoral council. By gathering the parish community an initial direction is established, and the community of the parish takes part in choosing and empowering the members of the new pastoral council.

The second phase is developing a process which will keep the energy from stagnating or turning in on itself, as if the pastoral council, once established, had become an end in itself. The pastoral council carries the responsibility of the new collaborative leadership experience. Like the parish priest working on his own, the pastoral council can fall into the trap of working alone, serving the parish with great dedication, but without finding the ways of extending and pushing out the boundaries of empowerment and shared responsibility.

Just as the parish priest has to make a conscious decision to work with others in partnership, the pastoral council has to decide consciously and deliberately to create an ever-extending network of partnerships, inviting people to become involved in developing the life of the parish, and empowering them to take on responsibility and to share it in their turn. When people are involved like this as partners then they also have to make the same choices, always drawing more and more people into partnership until everyone is a part of the movement of service to others.

*Praise, appreciation and encouragement are the essential fuel of collaborative effort.*

The beginning of this process is to affirm all those already active in the parish. When a Pastoral Council is established, some active parishioners may get the impression that they are no longer needed: the Pastoral Council will take care of everything. They need to be reassured that they are needed and appreciated. Praise, appreciation and encouragement are the essential fuel of collaborative effort.

### Exploring new structures

Creative thought and energy has also to be put into exploring new structures for collaborative ministry. One of the ways in which a pastoral council can have an impact on parish development is by identifying key areas (guided by the insights received from the Questionnaire and Parish Assembly) and forming teams or working groups to explore what can be done to address these. Members of the pastoral council can lead these working groups and gather new members to work in partnership with them.

The mathematics of this exercise is quite striking. If there are 12 members in the pastoral council, 2 take on leadership of each of six working groups and each group gathers 10 parishioners, already there are 72 people applying their minds and energy for parish development on specific fronts – quite a biblical number, in fact!

| 2 CHOICES | | |
|---|---|---|
| Pastoral Council | OTHERS/PARTNERS | |
| | 2 CHOICES | |
| | HELPERS | PARTNERS |
| LEADERSHIP X 2 PER GROUP | | |
| 10 OTHER PARISHIONERS | | |
| 72 | | |

Since the 2 leaders are members of the pastoral council, there will be a natural link for feedback and communication when the pastoral council meets.

This kind of development cannot just be haphazard. It needs careful planning, and the operation of it should form part of the ongoing formation and training of the pastoral council and of the others involved. The training process will clarify the structures and the approach to each area of concern. It will also need to address the difficulties which can hold people back from becoming involved wholeheartedly in the renewal of the life of the parish.

Here are some of the difficulties which hold people back from this kind of participation:

1.  People are not used to it. For a long time in the Church people have been seen primarily as receivers of grace rather than as sources of grace. Practice of faith was often reduced to a minimum and the supply of this minimum was well covered because there were more than enough priests and religious. It is difficult to move away from that and see practice of faith as a whole way of life that needs everyone to contribute to its quality and beauty.

2.  Many people don't see that they have anything to contribute. (And maybe we see people that way also.) This can come from the poor self-image that so many people have. It can also come from comparing ourselves with others and thinking that we are less in terms of talents, education, possessions etc. We then cannot see the unique gifts each of us brings to life. In 1979 Pope John Paul II, speaking in the Phoenix Park in Dublin, stated: *'there is no such thing as an "ordinary" lay person.'* Unfortunately in practice so many of our people don't really believe this. True pastoral care has to mean finding the ways of helping every person in the parish to believe this truth about herself/himself and so enable everyone to take their rightful place in the evangelisation of the world.

3.  Another difficulty that is often there for people in responding generously to the invitation to serve is their condition of life. Some think of themselves as too old. Of course when people get old they are not capable of much of what they used to do. That does not mean they are capable of

nothing. Far from it. Old age brings with it its own gifts and these are badly needed in every community. Others can be seen as too young. The reality is that the newly born/baptised baby has gifts for the community and these can be called on. They say that parents wait anxiously for the first year for their baby's first word, first step –and then spend the next 20 years telling them to sit down and shut up! We can be like that as God's family also. We strongly and beautifully promote the dignity of human life from conception. But when a baby is born we can often behave as if she/he is a nuisance. Right through the years from birth to death every person carries with them special gifts to enrich the Church. Our task is to help find the many and varied ways by which these can be made available.

Another condition of life that often becomes a block for people is sickness. Our Catholic tradition is one of the few, or maybe only, sources of wisdom that teaches us that sickness can contribute to human salvation. We have the special Sacrament of Anointing the Sick which is a powerful prayer for the sick person. This Sacrament is also a claiming of the sickness in a person's life to fill out what is lacking in the sufferings of Christ for the salvation of the world. It's not that God wants us to suffer. Suffering and pain are a normal part of the human condition, a part that does not have to make us useless but can become a very powerful part of our contribution to our world.

4. Many people are increasingly busy in their lives and this is certainly a block to service of others. It is said that if you want something done ask a really busy person. Today many are not really busy because they are busy about so many unimportant things. The really busy person is one who has priorities and can make time for other important things. For the sake of our physical and mental health it is vital today to make time for a marriage relationship, for family building, for prayer, for service to those in need. Without making that time people get themselves into all kinds of life messes.

5. Of course, today the very serious issues in the Church make it very difficult for a lot of people to get involved with others. This is particularly true of the terrible scandal of child sex abuse which has totally alienated some people and almost paralysed others with shock and with anger. This, and other

issues in the life of the Church, such as the role of women, need to be faced honestly and humbly by us together so that they are not allowed to destroy in us the power of God's Spirit.

6. Possibly the worst block of all to people's involvement in ministry in the Church and in the mission of the Church to the world is the fact that we don't believe enough in the goodness of each person. When this lack of belief is present in our priests or in the members of a Pastoral Council the result is that people are not asked, or only the safe people are asked. The experience of life is that in giving we receive. By inviting individual people to be partners with us in the pastoral care of our parishioners we are truly offering them a precious gift. We cannot demand that any person would accept the gift. But we can keep offering, believing that with every person who is not involved we are all the poorer and those people themselves will not know the full joy of human life.

*By inviting individual people to be partners with us in the pastoral care of our parishioners we are truly offering them a precious gift.*

Of course, different people will wish to participate in different ways, and we should respect that. Some people will respond to the challenge of sharing in a new collaborative leadership. They will enjoy contributing to decision making and new developments in the parish. Others, at particular times, will be willing to be involved, but not as partners with shared responsibility. For the moment they are happy to be helpers in whatever work needs to be done, leaving the policy decisions to others. That is fine. Every parish needs many helpers, and there is always the freedom to move between roles: someone who is a helper today may be a partner in responsibility tomorrow, and vice versa.

### Beyond the Parish Boundary

The parish pastoral council operates within the local parish community. But like the parish itself, it doesn't exist in isolation. It is part of the wider community of the diocese. The pastoral council depends on the diocese for support and management. It also draws inspiration and support from other parish pastoral councils and from a network of contacts at diocesan, regional and national level.

### Diocesan policy and support structures

Many dioceses have clearly defined policies on parish pastoral councils. Some of these are posted on the diocesan website on the internet. Some, like Dublin's, are published in book form. This can be a great support to an individual parish in developing a pastoral council. More importantly, perhaps, it can ensure continuity and consistency. If a diocesan policy exists, it is less likely that a pastoral council can be dropped when a new parish priest is appointed. The expectation will be established that a pastoral council is the norm in every parish.

A diocesan policy can be developed using the formulations of policy from Vatican II, *Christifideles Laici* and papal statements from Paul VI to Pope John Paul II. It can be given appropriate local application with the help of local laity, priests and religious, and the policy can be spelled out in the form of practical guidelines.

As well as policy and guidelines, a diocese can assist parishes in this kind of development by having a diocesan office (like Dublin's Pastoral Resource Office) or at least a resource person with whom parishes can liaise. The diocese can facilitate training and formation, either directly, or by encouraging parishes to participate in shared initiatives. Diocesan support and encouragement could be expressed by having an annual Day for Pastoral Councils.

### Regional and national resources

Parishes can link into facilities and initiatives at regional and national level, such as the National Conference of Priests' conferences at national and regional level, which have often addressed issues like collaborative ministry. Training and facilitation can be accessed also beyond the boundaries of the local parish or diocese.

### Clustering of Parishes

Sharing of facilities between parishes is becoming more frequent, and there is increasing talk of 'clustering of parishes', though that can mean different things in different places.

If it is true that the purposes of a parish are to gather people to worship and pray, to support and develop the faith of each other, and to proclaim Christ's salvation to the world, then we need to examine what we mean when we talk of clustering parishes. There is no doubt that we have the beginning of a crisis in relation to the number of priests in most dioceses in the Western world. And that crisis extends to the relatively small numbers of new possible vocations in our seminaries. Obviously this creates the need for a fresh approach to all that we do. Many dioceses see this fresh approach in the clustering of three or four parishes which would be served from a pool of two or three priests. This could certainly cater for the availability of worship through the Eucharist. But it could also lead to a lessening of the possibility of support for one another in faith as parishes lose their identity and become absorbed in a large conglomerate.

Instead of talking about clustering parishes maybe we should be talking about clustering priests. Their task then is to find the best ways of being at the service of the various parish communities that are in their care. The priests' main contribution to these parishes, but not by any means their only one, is the celebration of Mass. New forms of infrastructure need to be developed to cater for the needs and the growth of these parishes. Instead of thinking of a number of parishes being brought together and losing their identity, we can think of new creative ways of giving these parishes fresh impetus through the gifts and talents that exist among their people. These gifts are certainly there for administration. But they are also there for pastoral care. This approach could well ultimately lead us to a fresh thinking about deployment of priests and help us to get beyond the crisis mentality into a positive and energetic empowerment of the local Catholic community. A vibrant community can then interact with neighbouring parish communities and with the priests appointed to the area. People who used to passively await the ministry of the priest can take on a new and active way of being Catholic and help us to get beyond the crisis.

A core value of successful clustering is partnership. If we approach clustering from a mentality of scarcity or poverty, then there will be a competitive spirit and a smaller parish will inevitably lose out. But if we approach it from a mentality of abundance, then each parish will contribute in proportion to its resources, and bring to the partnership its gifts and traditions and its own identity. The more vibrant the parish community is, large or small, the more the parishioners take responsibility for their own faith community and its growth, the more it will grow and develop. Where there is genuine partnership and collaboration, everyone will benefit.

*Evaluation*

In chapter 1 we asked how it could be that there isn't a pastoral council in every parish and in every diocese. There is obvious encouragement and even exhortation at the highest policy level in the Church. There is a growing body of experience in Ireland and in other countries. There is the very nature of the Church, calling for all the baptised and confirmed to be given their true role and full responsibility in the life of the faith community.

A lot of books are appearing on collaborative ministry and on pastoral councils and a new approach to leadership and service in the Church. It's like an idea whose time has come. Yet it is not easy to maintain the energy that is required to develop new ways of doing things. Working together may be a better way, but it is not a faster way of doing business. A parish priest might well conclude: it will be quicker if I do it myself, and many people will be quite happy to watch him do it.

It is only in retrospect that we can really begin to assess the value of what has been happening. It is important to build in a process of review or assessment, to look at the experience, to affirm what is effective and fruitful, and to redirect what is off the mark. Even the simple process of noting the key dates in the development process in the parish, and writing down the sequence of events, can give an idea of how much has actually taken place, and the significance of each stage and of each landmark event.

In Ardmore, Co. Derry, we began our process of development in 1999-2000. The key dates were:

| | |
|---|---|
| *Advent 1999* | Lead in to Jubilee Year (diocesan guidelines) |
| *January 2000* | Celebration Liturgy; |
| *Easter 2000* | The faith community celebrates; looking ahead to parish mission; |
| *May 2000* | Parish Mission, led by Fr Johnny Doherty CSsR (family roots in Ardmore). |
| | On final weekend of Mission, questionnaire at all Masses. Festival Day. |

| | |
|---|---|
| *June/July 2000* | Professional Analysis of responses to Questionnaire (Research and Evaluation Services, Belfast). |
| *September 2000* | Summary of responses sent to each home, with letter of invitation to weekend Parish Assembly. |
| *14–15 October 2000* | Parish Assembly facilitated by Fr Johnny Doherty and Frank Dolaghan. |
| *7 November 2000* | Meeting in church, facilitated by Fr Johnny Doherty and Frank Dolaghan. |
| *November/ December 2000* | Setting up Pastoral Council (area elections etc.) |
| *Advent–Easter* | Induction Process for Pastoral Council, including overnight Retreat-Reflection in St Clement's, Belfast. |
| *Holy Week 2001* | Guided by Fr Johnny Doherty: Outdoor celebrations of the Word; Walk with the Cross, etc. Washing of the Feet as a commissioning to serve: parish priest washes feet of pastoral council members, who then in turn wash the feet of others through the congregation. |
| *Jan – May 2002* | Six monthly meetings: induction process for Pastoral Council, stage 2, leading to water-jar groups. |
| *2003* | Development of water-jar groups, each led by 2 pastoral council members. |
| *Holy Week 2003* | |
| *October 2003* | Review weekend for water-jar groups. |
| *Holy Week 2004* | |
| *May 2004* | Second Mission/Festival Day |
| *October 2004* | Second Parish Assembly |

*'The whole parish community is called together as the pilgrim people of God and as the Body of Christ.'*

Listing the key events has a value, and gives a sense of overview. But there is also need for a deeper kind of review and analysis. For example, a significant landmark in developing the pastoral council in Ardmore was the setting up of six working groups (which we called 'water jar' groups in the light of the marriage feast of Cana). Two pastoral council members led each group, and gathered other people into the group. The idea was to plan and develop initiative in the areas of community building, marriage and family life, youth, social issues, ecumenism and empowerment of the laity. It was a big step, and we had no existing template to work from. It really was a trial and error exploration. Some groups would develop more quickly; some perhaps slightly off course, or uneasy about what they should be doing. The groups had been formed in the beginning of 2002. In October 2003 we had a review weekend, giving each group an opportunity to assess progress.

The review of the groups had a twofold focus:

1. to clarify together the purpose of the group in the context of the wider vision for the parish;

2. to discuss and choose appropriate projects and to plan ahead.

*That everyone would catch the vision and enjoy following it.*

The response of the groups was remarkably similar. They wanted reassurance about the value of what they were doing. They wanted to locate their efforts in the context of the other groups and of the wider parish vision. They wanted to renew energy and enthusiasm. They acknowledged the need to communicate regularly with the full parish community. The groups were asked to reflect on 'one thing I would like to see'. A number of practical suggestions surfaced. The facilitator expressed the very positive desire 'that everyone would catch the vision and enjoy following it.'

The review of the groups was an important occasion, a self-assessment and renewal of purpose and energy. A broader based review of the whole process of development took place in 2004, a transition year for the pastoral council.

The parish pastoral council was structured for continuity as well as change. The idea was to renew the membership on a four year cycle. Out of 12 members, 3 would retire each year, after the initial term, and be replaced. Since the process began in the year 2000, it was appropriate to review it in 2004. Holy week 2004 was a good experience, with the involvement of many people in the various celebrations, including the outdoor Walk with the Cross on Good Friday and the Dawn Mass on Easter Sunday morning. In May 2004 we had a second Parish Mission, designed to continue the process of involving people in the life of the parish. In November 2004 we held a second Parish Assembly.

The Parish Assembly didn't begin well. It was in the school assembly hall, the weather was cold, and less than 20 people turned up. We were tempted to cancel, but decided to go ahead. A few more people arrived, and as soon as things got under way, the atmosphere began to build up. Those present first addressed the question: **What changes have you seen in the parish over the past four years?** It was when people wrote what had struck them and then talked about it that we began to realise how much had happened. More than that, what had happened had affected those who lived through it to a much greater extent than we had realised: there was a sense of satisfaction and even excitement.

The first change which people noted concerned communication. They had experienced more discussion. They felt that 'people have a voice'. They had a sense of new beginnings, that 'seeds had been planted'. Very significantly, they felt that over the four years there was an acceptance of change. It was like an affirmation of the vision statement from the first parish assembly, which included the marvellous phrase: 'to have the courage to invoke change'.

The members of the parish pastoral council obviously had a particular experience of growth and development. They had gained confidence. They had benefited enormously from their own overnight retreat with the neighbouring parish pastoral council of Culmore, Derry. Meeting people from other parishes at the Northern Region and national NCPI conferences had given them a wider vision of the Church. They welcomed the guidance of facilitators, who had enabled priest and people to learn and to explore together.

Over the four years they were struck by the increase in the number of people actively involved in the parish. Ardmore already had a tradition of participation, but there was more involvement of lay people now than ever, including the six working groups ('water jar groups') associated with the pastoral council. There were the young people, in roles like 'welcomers' at Mass. There was the Nazareth Group (Confirmation and post-confirmation programme), the Junior Pioneers, the experience of the Youth Mass and the Youth Retreat at Easter 2004.

The Church had been the focus for a lot of creativity, with the colourful 'Easter Garden' and the variety of developments round

Holy Week. The young people's liturgies also added colour and vitality. Special occasions like the Mass for the Bereaved in November involved many people. Participation in occasional Eucharistic Services was also appreciated. Groups like St. Joseph's Young Priest's Society and the Continuous Prayer Movement for Marriage and Family Life involved people not only in the Church, but in their personal and family prayer. The use of CB radio link brought the Mass and parish life to the sick and housebound. Pilgrimages to Knock and to the Clonard Novena in Belfast were appreciated as opportunities for doing things together and strengthening the sense of a living faith community.

The development of a parish is about people rather than about buildings, but there was a sense of satisfaction about the new service building for the cemetery, and about the planning of a parish pastoral resource centre to cater for the various active groups and to provide a parish meeting place.

It is in listing these things that we realise that a lot has happened. In day to day experience it seems to happen very slowly. There were times when pastoral council members felt impatient, and perhaps frustrated. But one member, during a session of the six month induction process, shared a valuable insight. Anne Marie had just had a new baby. 'I thought the nine months of waiting was just so that the baby could grow and be able to survive in the world,' she said, 'but then I realised that Edward and I needed the time to grow as well, so that we could be ready to look after this new life and accept all the change and disruption to our routine that it would invoke'. Then she added: 'When we started these meetings of the pastoral council, I was impatient. I wanted to see things happening. I was frustrated by all this reflection and prayer and Scripture and talk. But now I realise that as a pastoral council we needed this time to grow also, just like us as parents getting ready for our child'. It was a lovely moment of insight.

It was when people looked beyond the changes and activities to respond to the question: **What impact have these changes had on us and on the parish?** that the most important sharing took place. It was then that the extent of growth and the maturity of reflection became apparent. Beyond a new interest in what goes on in the parish, beyond the desire to become personally involved, beyond knowing where to go to find information or to share insights, beyond realising how much

*People had moved from being a consumer to being a participant, from waiting for things to happen to wanting to make them happen.*

more is to be done and how exciting is the challenge of doing it, people at the second parish assembly talked of the change that had taken place in themselves. Attitudes on basic things like what it means to be Catholic had changed. People had moved from being a consumer to being a participant, from waiting for things to happen to wanting to make them happen. Some things had already happened. Others were in process. There was a desire for better and deeper relationships with other churches. There was a desire for more involvement of young people, and a growing realisation of the importance of our young people. There was an interest in meeting other groups and sharing experiences and looking outward. There was pride and hope and the confidence that we can do things.

The value of parish development, and the value of working at it through the parish pastoral council, goes way beyond any activity or achievement. Through the effort at involvement, many more people are experiencing shared leadership in the Church. A wider pool of people are taking on responsibility, being empowered by their community for the sake of their community, and learning to work together in trust and accountability. It all happens slowly, little step by little step. Think big, act small. We couldn't find better words to sum it up than the words of Archbishop Oscar Romero:

> *We accomplish in our lifetime only a tiny fraction*
> *of the magnificent enterprise that is God's work.*
> *Nothing we do is complete, which is another way of saying*
> *that the Kingdom always lies beyond us.*
>
> *No statement says all that could be said.*
> *No prayer fully expresses our faith.*
> *No confession brings perfection.*
> *No pastoral visit brings wholeness.*
> *No programme accomplishes the Church's mission.*
> *No set of goals and objectives includes everything.*
>
> *That is what we are about.*
> *We plant a seed that will one day grow.*
> *We water seeds already planted,*
> *knowing that they hold future promise.*
> *We lay foundations that will need further development.*
> *We provide yeast that produces effects far beyond our capabilities.*

*We cannot do everything*
*and there is a sense of liberation in realising that.*
*This enables us to do something and to do it very well.*

*It may be incomplete, but it is a beginning, a step along the way,*
*an opportunity for the Lord's grace to enter and do the rest.*

*We may never see the end results, but that is the difference between*
*the master builder and the worker.*
*We are workers, not master builders, ministers, not messiahs.*

*We are prophets of a future not our own.*

**Resources**

**Parish Prayer**

*O Jesus,*
*help us to make you*
*the centre of our lives.*

*Help us to repent*
*of the wrongs we have done,*
*that we may be refreshed in spirit*
*and renewed in hope.*

*Help us to be good to one another*
*and to be faithful to you,*
*as we live out our vocations:*
*married, single, priest, religious –*
*so that our homes and our parish*
*may be filled with your presence*
*and be powerful sources*
*of your peace.*
*Amen.*

**Sample Mission Plan**

The following draft plan is given as an example, to indicate
possibilities. It covers 2 weekends and the intervening week,
including 2 morning Masses, an evening session, and various
paraliturgies or special Masses.

The first weekend involves an introduction to the Mission by the
Mission team at all Masses, with a special Mass and/or opening
session of the Mission on the Sunday afternoon or evening.

On the weekdays of the Mission week, two sets of themes are
developed, one at the morning Masses, and one at each of the
evening sessions.

**MONDAY:**
**Masses – The Purpose of the Mass**
The Mass is not for spectators or customers waiting to be served,
but calls us to be involved as a community of faith, building each
other up as members of the Body of Christ.

**Evening Session: Christ at the centre of our lives**
Scripture Mt 16:13 -20. Who do you say I am?
Our experience of Church begins with knowing Jesus Christ and learning to respond to him as disciples.

**TUESDAY:**
**Masses – The Penitential Rite**
Forgiveness is emphasised at the beginning of Mass, but also in the Our Father, at Communion time, and at the very heart of the Consecration. God forgives us, and calls us to forgive each other: without this we can't have genuine Christian community.

**Evening Session: Our Vocation as Followers of Christ**
Scripture Mt 17: 1-8. The Transfiguration
We are a called and calling Church: called to belong and called to serve.

**WEDNESDAY:**
**Masses – The Liturgy of the Word**
The word of God opens up for us the reality of who we are as God's people and the disciples of Jesus. We are nourished by the word and guided into living the Gospel way of life, a life of unity, in contrast with the individualism of the world.

**Evening Session – A Sinful People**
Scripture Mt 18: 1-5. Unless you change
We are called to change, not just because we are sinners, but because we are disciples. In our weakness and sinfulness, we are called to bring the reality of our lives into the project of building the Kingdom of God.

**THURSDAY:**
**Masses – The Liturgy of the Eucharist**
We are nourished into unity in the Body of Christ. Because the bread is one, we though many are one body because we partake of the one bread.

**Evening Session: A Forgiven People**
Scripture Lk 15: 11-32. The Prodigal Son
We are sinners who are loved. The Father waits for us with open arms. We also are called to forgive each other, to be a people of forgiveness. This is celebrated this evening in the

Sacrament of Reconciliation. Without forgiveness, we cannot build community.

## FRIDAY:
### Masses – The Communion Rite
*'The Body of Christ. Amen.'* The twofold profession of faith: Yes, this is the Body of Christ, Jesus here with us in Communion, but also: yes, we are the Body of Christ; we become what we receive. We reverence one another as we reverence Jesus in his Eucharistic presence. (St Augustine).

### Evening Session – A People with a Mission
**Scripture** Mt 28: 16–20. Go, make disciples
We are sent out to make disciples by the way we treat one another. We are a sacramental community, living a way of life which makes it possible for our young people who are baptised and confirmed and receive the Eucharist to grow in love and energy without being submerged in the selfish consumer culture of the world. By the way we live, we reassure them that Jesus is with us and with them always, to the end of time.

## SATURDAY:
### Mass for the Sick
We claim the pain and suffering of our sick and elderly to fill out what is lacking in the sufferings of Christ through the Sacrament of Anointing. We witness that we are a community where our sick are accompanied on their journey in hope, and those who care for them do not feel abandoned.

Questionnaire/Survey

A Sample Questionnaire from St Mary's, Ardmore, Derry (see over the page).

A Sample Questionnaire from

## ST MARY'S, ARDMORE, DERRY

This questionnaire is meant to encourage a process of reflection on the life and future of our parish as a living faith community. Your answers will be carefully considered and will help identify the priorities to be addressed in the future.

## 1. RELATIONSHIPS AND INVOLVEMENT IN THE PARISH

Please think about each of the following and **circle the phrase** which **best** describes your view:

| | | | | | |
|---|---|---|---|---|---|
| The quality of relationships between priests and people is... | Excellent[1] | Good[2] | Fair[3] | Poor[4] | Don't Know[5] |
| Relationships between the people and the schools are... | Excellent[1] | Good[2] | Fair[3] | Poor[4] | Don't Know[5] |
| The work of parish organisations is... | Excellent[1] | Good[2] | Fair[3] | Poor[4] | Don't Know[5] |
| Cooperation between parish organisations is... | Excellent[1] | Good[2] | Fair[3] | Poor[4] | Don't Know[5] |
| Involvement of women in the parish is... | Excellent[1] | Good[2] | Fair[3] | Poor[4] | Don't Know[5] |
| Involvement of men in the parish is... | Excellent[1] | Good[2] | Fair[3] | Poor[4] | Don't Know[5] |
| The process of decision making in the parish is... | Excellent[1] | Good[2] | Fair[3] | Poor[4] | Don't Know[5] |
| Involvement of youth in the parish is... | Excellent[1] | Good[2] | Fair[3] | Poor[4] | Don't Know[5] |
| The level and range of parish based social activities is... | Excellent[1] | Good[2] | Fair[3] | Poor[4] | Don't Know[5] |
| Relationships with other Christian churches locally are... | Excellent[1] | Good[2] | Fair[3] | Poor[4] | Don't Know[5] |
| Support for families in the parish is... | Excellent[1] | Good[2] | Fair[3] | Poor[4] | Don't Know[5] |
| Support for bereaved people is... | Excellent[1] | Good[2] | Fair[3] | Poor[4] | Don't Know[5] |
| Support for elderly people is... | Excellent[1] | Good[2] | Fair[3] | Poor[4] | Don't Know[5] |
| Support for people with disabilities is... | Excellent[1] | Good[2] | Fair[3] | Poor[4] | Don't Know[5] |
| Support for sick people is... | Excellent[1] | Good[2] | Fair[3] | Poor[4] | Don't Know[5] |
| Support for marriages in difficulties is... | Excellent[1] | Good[2] | Fair[3] | Poor[4] | Don't Know[5] |
| Support for teenagers and young people is... | Excellent[1] | Good[2] | Fair[3] | Poor[4] | Don't Know[5] |
| Support for single adults in the parish is... | Excellent[1] | Good[2] | Fair[3] | Poor[4] | Don't Know[5] |
| Relationships among parishioners are... | Excellent[1] | Good[2] | Fair[3] | Poor[4] | Don't Know[5] |

## 2. SACRAMENTS IN THE PARISH

Please consider each of the following and **circle the phrase** which **best** describes your views:

| | | | | |
|---|---|---|---|---|
| Baptism arrangements and support | No change needed[1] | Could be improved[2] | Must be changed[3] | Unable to Comment[4] |
| First Holy Communion arrangements | No change needed[1] | Could be improved[2] | Must be changed[3] | Unable to Comment[4] |
| Arrangements for Confirmation | No change needed[1] | Could be improved[2] | Must be changed[3] | Unable to Comment[4] |
| Support for Marriage Preparation | No change needed[1] | Could be improved[2] | Must be changed[3] | Unable to Comment[4] |
| Arrangements for Marriage | No change needed[1] | Could be improved[2] | Must be changed[3] | Unable to Comment[4] |
| Support for Couples after Marriage | No change needed[1] | Could be improved[2] | Must be changed[3] | Unable to Comment[4] |
| Arrangements for Funerals | No change needed[1] | Could be improved[2] | Must be changed[3] | Unable to Comment[4] |
| Arrangements for Sacrament of the Sick | No change needed[1] | Could be improved[2] | Must be changed[3] | Unable to Comment[4] |
| Times of Sunday Masses | No change needed[1] | Could be improved[2] | Must be changed[3] | Unable to Comment[4] |
| Participation by Lay people in Masses | No change needed[1] | Could be improved[2] | Must be changed[3] | Unable to Comment[4] |

## 3. PARISH RESOURCES

Please give your view on each statement below by circling **Yes, No** or **Unable to comment**

| | | | |
|---|---|---|---|
| I consider the involvement of the Laity is an essential part of Parish Life | Yes[1] | No[2] | Unable to comment[3] |
| I would be prepared to become more involved in the work of the parish | Yes[1] | No[2] | Unable to comment[3] |
| I am well informed about parish activities, events and news | Yes[1] | No[2] | Unable to comment[3] |
| I find the weekly bulletin helpful | Yes[1] | No[2] | Unable to comment[3] |
| I contribute regularly to church collections | Yes[1] | No[2] | Unable to comment[3] |
| I am eligible for and have entered the Covenant Scheme | Yes[1] | No[2] | Unable to comment[3] |
| I understand how and where my contributions are being used | Yes[1] | No[2] | Unable to comment[3] |

Please use the space below if you have any specific comments about **Parish Resources**:

_____

_____

_____

## 4. THE PARISH IN THE FUTURE

By the year 2005 I would like to see: *(Please tick the items you consider important)*

An Active Parish Pastoral Council ❑

Adult Religious Education Programmes ❑

Supports for Marriage and Family Life ❑

Widespread Family Prayer ❑

Involvement of Youth in the life of the Church ❑

Links with other Christian Churches locally ❑

Greater involvement of people in Parish Organisations ❑

A Vibrant Parish Community which:

• Deepens Faith ❑

• Hands on the Faith ❑

• Encourages all Vocations ❑

• Is an Inclusive Community ❑
  (Gender, social status, age, etc.)

• Is a caring community ❑
  (local needs and e.g. Third World)

Add other suggestions:

_____
_____
_____
_____
_____

**5. A LITTLE ABOUT YOU**: please circle each answer which applies to you.

| | | | |
|---|---|---|---|
| Are you: | | Male[1] | Female[2] |

| | | | |
|---|---|---|---|
| Are you a native of Ardmore Parish | | Yes[1] | No[2] |

If you answered **No**, how many years have you lived in the Parish? _____

Your Age       Between 12 and 18[1]    Between 19 and 30[2]
                              Between 31 and 55[3]    Between 56 and 70[4]    Over 70[5]

| | | | | |
|---|---|---|---|---|
| Do you attend Weekday Masses | Never[1] | Seldom[2] | Often[3] | Every Day[4] |
| Do you attend Sunday Mass | Never[1] | Seldom[2] | Often[3] | Every Day[4] |

| | | |
|---|---|---|
| Do you feel you belong to this parish? | Yes[1] | No[2] |
| Are you a member of any Parish Organisation? | Yes[1] | No[2] |
| Are there any issues which are making it difficult for you to belong as a member of our Parish Community? | Yes[1] | No[2] |

**Please circle your answer if any of the following apply to you**

| | | |
|---|---|---|
| I am in a relationship which is not recognised by the Church | Yes[1] | No[2] |
| There are some parts of the teachings of the Church with which I am uncomfortable | Yes[1] | No[2] |
| As a woman, I feel undervalued in the Church | Yes[1] | No[2] |
| I have experienced hurt in the Church at some time and this has not been healed | Yes[1] | No[2] |

### Thank you for your help

This questionnaire has been completed mainly at the weekend Masses 27 - 28 May. If you have completed it at home, please return it to the Sacristy or to Fr Crilly, Fr McQuillan or Sr Teresa as soon as possible. Thank you.

**Sample Outcomes from Survey**

### PARISH IN FUTURE

| | |
|---|---|
| Active parish pastoral council | Yes 64% |
| Adult religious education programmes | Yes 47% |
| Support for marriage/family life | Yes 76% |
| Widespread family prayer | Yes 68% |
| Youth involved in life of church | Yes 85% |
| Links with other churches | Yes 68% |
| People more involved | Yes 73% |
| Vibrant parish which deepens faith | Yes 69% |
| Vibrant parish which hands on faith | Yes 56% |
| Vibrant parish which encourages all vocations | Yes 69% |
| Vibrant inclusive parish community | Yes 70% |
| Vibrant caring parish community | Yes 87% |

### PARISH RESOURCES

| | |
|---|---|
| Involvement of laity essential | Yes 77% |
| Prepared to become more involved | Yes 54% |
| Well informed | Yes 71% |
| Bulletin helpful | Yes 93% |
| Contribute regularly | Yes 86% |
| Eligible for and involved in Covenant Scheme | Yes 44% |
| Understand how contributions are being used | Yes 70% |

## Invitation to Parish Assembly

Dear Parishioner,

Our Parish Mission last May was the beginning of a process. Thank you for entering into that experience so wholeheartedly. Thanks to all of you for taking the time to fill in the Questionnaires for the Parish Survey. This booklet gives a summary of your responses – it actually gives your response to all the questions in percentage form, but without the breakdown by age, gender etc. That can be had from the full book of the survey, as analysed by Research and Evaluation Services.

We are now approaching the next step in the process, which is our Parish Assembly – an opportunity for parishioners to get together and reflect on the results of the Survey, and on the life of the parish generally.

On Saturday the 14th and Sunday the 15th of October you are welcome to join in a weekend of prayer and reflection, of discernment and planning for the development of the parish over the next few years. We are lucky that Ardmore has a great tradition of faith and of involvement in the parish. It is important for us to build on that.

The leadership team for the Parish Assembly will consist of Fr Johnny Doherty CSsR, and Frank and Aileen Dolaghan. Frank and Aileen have facilitated a similar process for the parish of Newry.

The weekend will run as follows *(it is very important to attend for the whole weekend)*:
    **Saturday, 14 October:**     **11.00am until 4.00pm, including a light lunch.**
    **Sunday, 15 October:**     **2.30pm until 7.00pm, including a light tea.**

The working part of the Assembly will take place in the Beech Hill House Hotel. On Saturday night we will gather for a Parish Social Evening in McCourt's Bar.

To help in giving us an indication of the numbers attending, please fill in the form below.

Thank you. I look forward to seeing you there.


Fr Oliver Crilly PP

---

*I hope to attend the Ardmore Parish Assembly*


Name: _____


Address: _____

_____

## ST MARY'S ARDMORE
## PARISH ASSEMBLY
## AGENDA

**SATURDAY**

| | |
|---|---|
| 11.00am | Opening Prayer<br>Welcome; Introductions<br>Expectations; Guidelines |
| 11.15am | Where are we now?<br>Looking at our survey, which are the three most important things which have emerged? |
| 12.00 noon | What kind of parish do we want? |
| 1.00pm | *Lunch* |
| 2.00pm | What are our goals or aims?<br><br>For each goal what objectives do we have?<br><br>For each objective what actions might we take? |
| 4.00pm | Review of the day<br>Agenda for tomorrow<br>Closing prayer |

**SUNDAY**

| | |
|---|---|
| 2.00pm | Opening Prayer; Welcome – Recap |
| 2.15pm | What resources do we have?<br>What resources do we need?<br>How and where will we get the resources? |
| 3.30pm | *Break* |
| 3.45pm | How will we organise ourselves to take forward the plan?<br><br>How will we ensure we bring the parish with us? |
| 5.00pm | Where do we go from here? |
| 5.30pm | Review of Assembly<br>Closing Prayer |

# 13. PASTORAL COUNCIL

## Election Documents

## ELECTIONS

The next stage in the process following the Parish Assembly is the formation of a new Parish Pastoral Council. Five members will be elected to represent the different areas of population in the Parish. Fr Crilly, Mgr McQuillan and Sr Teresa will be ex-officio members. Additional members may be co-opted, e.g. for gender balance, age balance, special expertise or experience, etc. up to a maximum of 12 members.

The election of area representatives will be in two stages. First, during the next two weeks, people from each area will be nominated for election. Nomination forms are given overleaf. Then the 3 most frequently nominated for each area will be included in the final voting paper. The final date for nominations will be Sunday, 26 November. Voting will be on 2 and 3 December.

NOTE:
1. To nominate or be nominated you must be 16 years of age or over.
2. You may nominate only one person, and that from your own area.
3. You may be nominated any number of times, as long as each nomination is by a different person.

## AREAS
A.  Ardmore/Goshaden (Rushall Road outwards);

B.  Currynierin/Tullyally/Church Road/Church Brae;

C.  Gleneen Park/Altnagelvin Park/Glenmore Park/Ashcroft/ out to the Glebe;

D.  Knightsbridge/Sevenoaks/Manor Wood

E.  Drumahoe/Cross Area
    (Daly's Park out through Drumahoe)

## NOMINATION FORMS

I hereby nominate: ..................................................................

Address: ..............................................................................
as a candidate for election to the Ardmore Pastoral Council.

Signed: ............................................. Date: ....................

Address: ..............................................................................

---

I hereby nominate: ..................................................................

Address: ..............................................................................
as a candidate for election to the Ardmore Pastoral Council.

Signed: ............................................. Date: ....................

Address: ..............................................................................

---

I hereby nominate: ..................................................................

Address: ..............................................................................
as a candidate for election to the Ardmore Pastoral Council.

Signed: ............................................. Date: ....................

Address: ..............................................................................

---

I hereby nominate: ..................................................................

Address: ..............................................................................
as a candidate for election to the Ardmore Pastoral Council.

Signed: ............................................. Date: ....................

Address: ..............................................................................

---

Note: The 3 names most frequently nominated for each area will be included in the final voting paper. The final date for nominations will be Sunday, 26 November. Voting will be on 2 and 3 December.

# VOTING PAPER

## ST MARY'S ARDMORE
### Pastoral Council Voting Paper

Place a mark opposite one name only – from your own area – to indicate the person you want to vote for. Do not add any other mark, or your paper will be invalid.

A. Ardmore/Goshaden (Rushall Road outwards):

❑ ............................................................................................................

❑ ............................................................................................................

❑ ............................................................................................................

B. Currynierin/Tullyally/Church Road/Church Brae:

❑ ............................................................................................................

❑ ............................................................................................................

❑ ............................................................................................................

C. Gleneen Park/Altnagelvin Pk/Glenmore Pk/Ashcroft/out to Glebe:

❑ ............................................................................................................

❑ ............................................................................................................

❑ ............................................................................................................

D. Knightsbridge/Sevenoaks/Manor Wood:

❑ ............................................................................................................

❑ ............................................................................................................

❑ ............................................................................................................

E. Drumahoe/Cross Area (Daly's Park out through Drumahoe):

❑ ............................................................................................................

❑ ............................................................................................................

❑ ............................................................................................................

Note: The names for each area should be listed in alphabetical order.

## INTRODUCTION

This six months formation programme consisting of a full day followed by five meetings, one per month, is mainly for a Parish Pastoral Council that is starting off. However, many elements of it are also valid for one that is already started. And many elements of it need to be repeated and renewed as a Parish Pastoral Council goes along. This is particularly true when new members join, which will be every year once the term of office begins to take effect. Every time a new member comes into any group, that group changes and this needs to be acknowledged.

## PURPOSES OF THE SIX MONTH FORMATION PROGRAMME

When a new Parish Pastoral Council is formed, the temptation is to get into taking action straight away. They see some urgent things to be done in the parish and they want to be seen to be doing them. The six months formation programme is a way of resisting this temptation and it needs to be resisted.

The purposes of the formation programme are many but all of them for the same reason, namely that the Parish Pastoral Council will be an effective leadership group for the whole parish community. The purposes are as follows:

1.  To get to know one another in ways that will shape the Parish Pastoral Council into a small community of faith. This involves learning to pray together; to be inspired by the Scriptures; to grow together in a love for the Church in their parish.

2.  To get to know what the Parish Pastoral Council is about, and what it is not about. This Council is not in place to take charge of the parish but to lead the charge in all that is needed to build the parish as an ever more vibrant community of faith.

3.  To plan together how they can best bring the work of the Assembly forward. This work will have produced a Vision Statement for the parish and also the beginnings of a Pastoral Plan. If the concepts in this book are being followed, the Pastoral Plan will be formed around the six development

areas which are referred to as the Six Water Jars.

4. To begin making decisions about specific leadership in each of these six development areas and who to invite to join them.

5. To make decisions about their on-going monthly meetings: suitable dates and times; procedures for their meetings; agenda setting; attendance commitment; and so on.

6. To elect a Chairperson, an assistant Chairperson, a Communications Secretary and an assistant Communications Secretary, while outlining clearly the responsibilities of each of these.

**SAMPLE OUTLINE FOR THE FULL DAY**

**9.30 – 10.00am** Welcome and introductions and prayer
Outline of the programme for the day – Facilitator.

**10.00 – 11.00am** Scripture: John 17 cf page 156 for thoughts for input
**1) What are the three things you like best about your parish?**
**2) Why are these important to you?**

Time to write answers
Small group sharing
Larger group sharing – use flipchart for these

**11.00 – 11.20am** Break

**11.20 – 12.30am** Continue reflection on John 17
**1) What three things would you like to see developed in the parish over the next 3 years?**
**2) What difference would each of these developments make to the parish community?**

Time to write answers
Small group sharing
Larger group sharing – flipchart

**12.30 – 1.30pm** Lunch

| 1.30 – 2.30pm | The Pastoral Council |
|---|---|

Continue reflection on John 17

**What do you see as the role of the pastoral Council in the future development of the parish?**

Time to write answers
Small group sharing
Larger group sharing

| 2.30 – 2.45pm | Break |
|---|---|

| 2.45 – 4.00pm | **The purposes of a Pastoral Council -** Cf page 52 |
|---|---|

for possible input

- Parish priest appointed to pastoral care of parishioners and to administration of parish
- Has two choices: can do it himself or can involve others
  Best practice is to involve others
- Now has two choices: can involve others as helpers or as partners. Helpers means things are more or less decided, they just need people to do them. Partners means involving others in discernment and decision-making.
  Best practice is to involve others as partners.
- A Parish Pastoral Council is a definite attempt at involving others as partners, specifically in the pastoral care of the parishioners.
- Once a Pastoral council is established it now has two choices: to do everything themselves or to involve others.
  Best practice is to involve others.
- Can choose to involve others as helpers or as partners.
  Best practice is to involve others as partners.
- This process keeps opening outwards until everyone is given an opportunity to be involved in the pastoral care of one another. The purpose of the Pastoral Council is to help move the parish to that point.

**1. What is your understanding of the purpose of the Pastoral Council now?**
**2. How can we best work together to make this Pastoral Council as effective as possible?**

Time to write answers
Small group sharing
Large group sharing

4.00 – 4.30pm    Sum up the day
**What three things have you heard or experienced here today that you think will be important for the development of this Pastoral Council?**

Time to write answers
Small group sharing
Larger group sharing – use flipchart for these

Conclude with some more reflection on John 17.

## MEETING 1

**Purpose:** to outline the six areas of development for the parish, that are referred to as the six waterjars, and to begin the process of sharing the leadership for these.

**Time: 7.30 – 9.30pm**

1.   Welcome and time for prayer

2.   Scripture: John 2. The wedding feast at Cana

3.   Input: cf p. 129 for material for this

Points to consider: do whatever he tells you. Three sources of the Word of God; Scripture, tradition and teaching of the Church, the world in which we live. As we listen to these three sources the six main areas to respond to are: Building Community; Ecumenism; Marriage and Family Life; Empowerment of the Laity; Social Issues; Involvement of Children and Young People.

Question:    **Using 1 as your first preference, how would you be willing to be involved in developing these six areas?**

Time to answer this question – by those elected or co-opted only. Ex officio members are available to whichever group needs them at particular times.

Sort out the six groups with at least two people in each group.

In their groups ask the question: **Who can we ask to join us in developing this area of pastoral care in the parish?** Each person writes down at least ten names first. Then they share their lists within their own small group. They then share their lists in the full group. In cases where more than one group has the names of the same people they negotiate as to who will ask each of these.

Having settled on their lists, each small group makes decisions about how they will go about asking each person and when.

Some of these decisions are then shared in the full group in order to encourage one another.

They have two months to complete their wider group as all these people are to be invited to the third of this series of meetings.

Encourage everyone to read up about the significance of their own group as outlined in pp. 132-46

Conclude with a prayer.


**MEETING 2**
**Purpose:** to grow in awareness of the importance of each of the six areas of pastoral care.

**Time: 7.30 – 9.30pm**

1.  Welcome and time for prayer

2.  Scripture: Mt 16. Who do people say the Son of Man is?
    Who do you say I am?

3.  Input: cf p. 116 for ideas

**Main point**: for now is to keep in mind that Christ is who we are about – his presence in the parish community and his power in every person for the transformation of the world. Without this focus people get caught into activity and settle for less than is possible.

4. **Task**:
   1) each small group to develop a 10 minute presentation on how they see their own area of concern and its relevance for the parish. Cf pp.132–46 for ideas on this. They should also include a response to the question: **what positive outcomes will there be for the parish as things begin to develop?**
   Take a half hour for this.

   2) Each small group to give their presentation to the full group with a few minutes each time for comment from the full group.

5. A reminder that the next meeting will include all their co-workers and so it is urgent that they keep asking.

   Finish with a prayer.


## MEETING 3
**Purpose**: to launch the six groups who will work on the six areas of pastoral care.

**Time: 7.30 – 9.30pm**

1. Welcome – people introduce themselves – time of prayer

2. Scripture: Mt 28. The five commands of Christ

3. Input: cf p. 165 for ideas

**Main point:** is to think big

4. Divide into the six groups – may need separate rooms for this.

5. **Task**:
   • Pastoral Council members to give the presentation they gave at last meeting to those they have gathered.

- List all that is already happening in the parish under their own heading

- What new projects could be developed under their heading?

- Who among themselves will take responsibility for each of these projects?

- Who will they involve, other than the people gathered here, in working on these projects?

- When will this small group meet next to continue this planning process?

**9.00 – 9.30pm** Gather all the groups together and have a large group sharing on how their meetings went and how they see the future development of their particular area of concern.

Conclude with a prayer.


## MEETING 4
**Purpose**: to look at the important elements that are necessary for the effectiveness of the Pastoral Council meetings and also their small group meetings.

**Time: 7.30 – 9.30pm**

1. Welcome and time of prayer

2. Scripture: Lk 24. The disciples on the Road to Emmaus

3. Input: cf p. 106 for ideas

**Main Point**: Meetings are opportunities for us to help each other meet Christ.

4. **Task**: to seek agreement on the main elements of the Pastoral Council's on-going meetings under the following headings:

**Frequency:** once a month with a full day each year to review the year ending and plan the year ahead. Agree on which day each month is best for everyone

**Duration:** the monthly meeting should last no longer than one and a half hours. Agree on a starting time and finishing time

**Agenda Setting:**

a) at this meeting do a brainstorm on what are the general things that should be on the agenda of the Pastoral Council? What are the general things that should not be on the agenda of the Pastoral Council?

b) Looking at the general things that should be on the agenda, list all those that will be put on the agenda for the next year.

c) Looking at this list, what items will be put on the agenda for the next three months? This list should be renewed each month.

*The principle of confidentiality is not about decisions, but about the people of the Pastoral Council. It is not about anything being secret but about everyone being sacred.*

**Attendance:** For a group like a Pastoral Council, attendance of everyone at all the meetings is vital. This helps the morale just as non-attendance lowers the morale. Obtain agreement on this and also on the procedures to be followed when someone cannot attend a meeting.

**Confidentiality:** One of the worst things that could happen to a Pastoral Council within a parish is that an air of secrecy be developed. The opposite should be the case where the parish is constantly being informed of all that is happening. The principle of confidentiality is not about decisions but about the people of the Pastoral Council. It is not about anything being secret but about everyone being sacred.

**Next Meeting:** Each month the last 15 minutes of the meeting should be dedicated to agreeing on the main points of the agenda for the next meeting. These are taken from what is left over from the present meeting; other items that are on the list for the next three months; other items that are on the list for the year. At the beginning of each meeting other items can be included under the heading of **AOB**.

These generally should be taken at the beginning of the meeting but left until the other agenda items have been covered.

5. End this meeting with an overview of all that has been agreed. This should then be drawn up into a form that each one will sign at the next meeting.

6. Finish with another short reflection on the Scripture reading and time of prayer.

## MEETING 5
**Purpose:** to elect people to particular offices of responsibility with the Pastoral Council.

**Time: 7.30 – 9.30pm**

1. Welcome and time of prayer

2. Scripture: Mt 17. The Transfiguration

3. Input: cf p. 147 for ideas

**Main Point:** *'Lord, it is wonderful for us to be here.'* This should be a feature of belonging to the Pastoral Council just as it should be a feature of belonging to the parish.

4. **Task:** to elect a Chairperson and assistant Chairperson; to elect a Communications Secretary and an assistant Communications Secretary. A note-taking secretary should be from outside the members of the Pastoral Council. This could be the parish secretary or someone else brought in for this specific purpose.

5. Elections are very important as they constitute a commitment of all the members to those they elect.

   a) Outline the responsibilities of the Chairperson. Have the election until someone is agreed upon.

   b) Outline the responsibilities of the assistant Chairperson. Have the election until someone is agreed upon.

c)  Outline the responsibilities of the Communications Secretary. Have the election until someone is agreed upon.

d)  Outline the responsibilities of the assistant Communications Secretary. Have the election until someone is agreed upon.

**N.B.** The parish priest is not eligible for any of these posts as he is already the president of the Pastoral Council. Any other ex officio members should also be avoided for these posts as their place is one of support for everyone else.

7.  Set the agenda for the next meeting, which will be a regular Pastoral Council meeting. This agenda is taken from the items agreed on for the next three months and any other items that were agreed on for the year. The number of items should be capable of being dealt with within one and a half hours, which always includes 15 minutes for setting the next agenda.

8.  Finish with another short reflection on the Scripture passage; a time of thanks for these six months; and a time of prayer.

## DRAFT CONSTITUTION

1.  **Name:**
    The Council shall be called 'St Mary's Ardmore Pastoral Council'.

2.  **Nature and Function:**
    2.1. The Parish Pastoral Council is a representative body of Christ's faithful whose purpose is the promotion of the mission of the Church in its entirety. Within the Pastoral Council, priests and people will work in close collaboration in matters pertaining to pastoral ministry.

    The function of the Pastoral Council is to deal with the mission of the Church, long-range and short-range goals and objectives, and to design those procedures and processes by which the pastoral work of the Church is to be accomplished.

2.2  In accordance with the Code of Canon Law (Canon536), the Council shall have a consultative voice. Through prayerful reflection and the guidance of the Holy Spirit 'who works in the world through the hearts of all who believe', the Pastoral Council will help to identify, implement and evaluate those pastoral initiatives and policies best suited to the spread of the gospel in this particular area.

3. **Membership:**

3.1  The Council shall consist of 10 to 15 members.

3.2  In so far as is possible, members should represent different areas of pastoral ministry, different geographical areas, women and men of different age groups and civil status (married, single, widowed, separated, divorced, students, senior citizens, etc.), people from different walks of life or social conditions.

3.3  Some members of the Council shall be ex officio (the priests of the parish and the parish sister).

3.4  Initially, not less than half the members shall be elected, and the remainder shall be co-opted in accordance with paragraph 3.2

4. **Officers:**

4.1  The parish priest shall be President of the Pastoral Council.

4.2  The Chairperson, whose function is the effective running of meetings, is elected by the members for a period of 2 years.

4.3  The Pastoral Council shall have a Communications Secretary, whose role is to keep in touch with the parish office and diocesan pastoral office, and facilitate regular communication with parishioners. *A note-taking secretary should be from outside the members of the Pastoral Council. This could be the parish secretary or someone else brought in for this specific purpose.*

4.4  For each of the posts in 4.2 and 4.3 a deputy will be elected, who will automatically take on the role in succession, at which time a new deputy will be elected.

5. **Meetings:**
   5.1 Meetings shall take place monthly, except for July and August. The parish priest, or another priest of the parish designated by him, shall be present at all meetings.

   5.2 The Agenda shall include matters pertaining to the mission of the Church, i.e. the full range of pastoral activities which will enable this particular faith community to listen more attentively to God's word and put it into practice in its day-to-day life.

   5.3 Because of the unique nature of the Council, a short period of each meeting shall be given to prayer and reflection on an appropriate section of God's word.

6. **Period of membership:**
   6.1 The period of office shall be 4 years. No member shall serve more than two consecutive terms but shall be eligible for re-nomination subsequently.

   6.2 After the initial term, three members shall retire each year in rotation.

   6.3 Any member failing to attend four consecutive meetings without reasonable explanation shall be deemed to have resigned.

   6.4 Mid-term vacancies shall be filled by co-option.

7. **Quorum:**
   A quorum shall consist of half the members of the Council.

8. **Sub-committees:**
   The Council may set up sub-committees to advise and assist it on matters of special pastoral concern. These would be made up of Pastoral Council members and others.

9. **Ongoing Formation of Members:**
   Study, reflection and in-service education on the nature and mission of the Church are an important element of the work of all Council members.

10. **Approval of the Constitution:**
    The norms of this Constitution are approved by the Bishop
    of the diocese.
    (*To be submitted.*)

11. **Cessation of Council:**
    Since it is advisory to the parish priest, the current Pastoral
    Council ceases to function when the post of parish priest
    becomes vacant.

**Note:** *The Archdiocese of Dublin guidelines make 2 valuable adjustments:*
*1. the inclusion of the Pastoral Council's vision statement; and*
*2. a transition year after the parish priest retires/dies.*

## 14. BOOKS AND MEDIA

*A Handbook for Parish Councils*, Jane Ferguson (Dublin Diocesan
    Guidelines). The Columba Press 2005

*Revisioning the Parish Pastoral Council, A Workbook*, Gubish,
    Jenny and McGannon, Paulist Press 2001.

*Pastoral Councils in Today's Catholic Parish*, Mark F. Fischer.
    Twenty-Third Publications 2001.

*The Welcoming Parish*, Donal Harrington. The Columba Press
    2005.

*The 7 Habits of Highly Effective People*, Stephen R. Covey. Simon
    & Schuster 1989, 1992, 1999.

*Parish Councils*, The Irish Council for the Apostolate of the
    Laity, Veritas Publications 1971.

*The Parish, a People, a Mission, a Structure*, National Conference
    of Catholic Bishops, USA, 1980.

*Pastoral Councils, Making Communion Visible*, Brendan Leahy,
    *Doctrine and Life*, April 2005.

*Ecclesiam Suam*, Pope Paul VI, Catholic Truth Society, London 1965, 1979.

The Vocation and Mission of the Laity (*Christifideles Laici*), Pope John Paul II, Veritas Publications, 1989.

*Familiaris Consortio*, The Christian Family in the Modern World, Pope John Paul II, Catholic Truth Society, London 1981.

*Novo Millennio Ineunte*, At the Beginning of the New Millennium, Pope John Paul II, Catholic Truth Society, London 2001.

*Partnership in Parish*, Enda Lyons, The Columba Press, 1987, 1988.

*Parish Renewal*, Donal Harrington, The Columba Press, 1997

*A Parish Pastoral Directory (Diocese of Ossory)*, Edited by William Dalton, The Columba Press 1995.

*Living the Sunday Liturgy*, Johnny Doherty CSsR, The Columba Press 1995.

## 15. OTHER USEFUL MATERIALS

### Love is for Life Trust

**Who we are**

Love is for Life Trust is a group of couples, priests, single people and religious who develop and promote programmes for the active support of married couples in their love for one another, and of families in their relationships with one another.

**What we believe**

We believe that the love of husband and wife is one of the greatest treasures of the Church and of society. It can also be one of the most fragile and in need of support. As Catholics we believe that this special relationship of the married couple is a Sacrament. That simply means that the sexual love of a man and woman in the committed relationship of marriage is one of the major ways that Christ is made present in our world for its salvation. What a wonderful belief!

**What are we committed to**
We are also fully committed to the belief that the family is where human life is lived at its best. Of course that doesn't happen automatically. It has to be made happen by the efforts of all to develop the qualities of love within the home. Some of these qualities are: joy, thanksgiving, praise, forgiveness, respect, freedom, prayer, good communication. We Catholics call the family the Domestic Church, the place where Christ lives through the love of family members. It's vital for the Church and for society that our families are given all the assistance possible to make their homes real places of life and love.

**Together Forever**

A set of five videos gives an excellent insight into marriage based on group meetings with Fr Johnny Doherty speaking and various couples relating their experiences, problems and solutions.

This unique input by couples and priest is a powerful tool which challenges and at the same time supports married couples. Fr Johnny's insight into marriage and the lived examples of the married couples allow those who participate in the programme to take time out and, if they wish, to re-evaluate their relationship.

The programme is designed so that it can be used by a couple on their own or by a number of couples who are happy to work together with a facilitator, perhaps in a parish.

**A Movement of Continuous Prayer**
**for Marriage and Family Life**

On 1 December 1998 the Movement of Continuous Prayer for Marriage & Family Life began. Since then there has been someone praying for marriage & family life at every moment. This was made possible by people taking on the commitment of a specific hour on a specific day each month in such a way that they were handing the prayer on to one another, much the same as a relay race!! Fr Johnny Doherty CSsR has written a special booklet to assist with this prayer so that the focus can be kept on marriage & family life for the full time. This Movement has now

spread to many places throughout the world and continues to spread every day. There are currently about 30,000 people involved with it. An annual day of prayer is held in Knock, Co. Mayo each October.

### The Nazareth Programme

Sr Carmel O'Shea OP produced this programme for young people aged 11-13. It is designed to help bridge the gap between Primary and Secondary Levels of education. It is a parish-based programme, conducted by a team from the parish but in conjunction with the schools. One of the aims is to help the young people keep in touch with the parish after they leave Primary school.

There are three modules in the programme. The first two of these take place between February and June of the final year in Primary school. The third takes place between September and November, the first three months of the Secondary level experience.

Retreats, weekly meeting content and format is presented in detail with templates for forms you may need. More on the Nazareth programme will be found in the Young people's section in the Family page on the Love is for Life website.

### Cana Weekend

Love is for Life Trust offers the Cana weekend to couples. This is a Scripture based weekend through which we reflect on the spirituality of marriage. If you would like to organise a group of couples for a weekend for this please get in touch with us and we will try to make appropriate arrangements. We also offer a day for couples that can be organised locally and we will try to supply a team for you.

### Engaged Couples Weekends

One of our major undertakings in Love is for Life Trust is working with couples preparing for marriage. It is a great joy and we have a very good residential programme for it. We have two centres going now – St Clement's, Belfast; Esker in Co. Galway.

## Make Me a Channel of your Peace

A programme for 15-16 year old young people, it is designed to be run by a married couple in their own home with a group of ten-twelve people. It is an exploration of all the significant relationships in the young people's lives at present and a preparation for the relationships that may become part of their lives in the future. Through this programme the young people experience the commitment of love and faith of the married couple and a single person and priest or religious who may be working with them. Lasting friendships are a feature of the programmes that have been run to date.

## Come and See
## A Parish Faith Development Programme

This Programme is an exploration of the life of faith we are called to as Catholics. It is suitable for those who are involved in the Church, those who are on the fringes, those who have given up, and new enquirers. It is designed as a series of meetings, with the possibility also of a weekend. It is Scripture-based and with a strong emphasis on small group sharing.

## Pastoral Council Training

We offer training in the principles and processes for Pastoral Councils as outlined in this book. This training can be for the whole package or for any of the individual parts of it. As our resources for this training are limited, planning ahead is very necessary. The training is on offer to individual parishes, any arrangement of a clustering of parishes, and a diocese.

## Parishioner Empowerment Weekend

When we think of involving people in the life and work of the parish we generally think first of the needs and then get people to cater for those. The Parishioner Empowerment Weekend is designed to look first at the gifts of each person and how those gifts could best be put at the service of the Community. The other people involved in the Weekend Programme make these decisions.

### Weekly Couple Prayer

Each week, under Couple Prayer, our website has a page for couples. It contains a short reflection based on the Gospel of the Sunday. This is followed by a short Morning Prayer, which is based on the Opening Prayer of the Sunday Mass; a Prayer during the Day, based on the Prayer Over the Gifts of the Sunday Mass; and an Evening Prayer, based on the Prayer After Communion of the Sunday Mass. There are then two questions for the week. The first of these is for the couple's own relationship; the second one is about general involvement in the community. There is also a Prayer Requests page in which people look for prayers for particular intentions.

### Family Prayer week by week

This programme is currently running only in the Parish of Ardmore, Derry. It can be made available to any other parish that is interested. Each week a sheet is given to each family with young children attending the Sunday Masses. On it is a Family Thought for the month, a Family Prayer for the week, and a Family Action for the week. There is also a blessing of the children by the parents and of the parents by the children for each night.

*For further information please contact:*

*johnnydoherty@utvinternet.com*

*www.loveisforlife.com*

# Part Two
## That the world may believe

# 16. ROOTED IN THE SCRIPTURES

The Parish Pastoral Council, like any other group, can easily get caught up in activity and forget the reason for this activity. The title of this book was chosen specifically to help this situation.

## 'Think Big'

The Scripture is our main source for our vision. And the prayer of Christ in John 17 gives us the ultimate point of that vision: 'that the world may believe'. This casts our eyes out to the horizon and opens our hearts to long for every person to come to know the love of God.

## 'Act Small'

The wonderful thing is that we don't have to save the world that we are looking at. Our task as followers of Christ is to make it possible for Christ to save our world. Every small action that helps to make his presence known contributes to this salvation. Every small step we take to enliven the parish community in faith, hope and love brings his salvation closer. Every person in the community that we can help to become more actively engaged in caring for others makes his salvation that little bit more visible.

## Particular Scripture Passages

In Part 2 we take six particular passages from the Gospels which can help us catch the spirit of adventure that a Pastoral Council needs to constantly renew. We give the text of these passages in full so that they can be read before going into the next part, 'Parish Implications'. In this part of each reflection we bring forward some of the important realities of our faith that can so easily get lost in activity. These Parish Implications give a wide scope of possibility for discussion at the Pastoral Council meetings and events.

## The Six Passages

### The Disciples on the Road to Emmaus (Luke 24:13-35)
This passage helps us to discover the six essential elements of a parish spirituality: Prayer, Scripture, Eucharist and other

Spirituality

Sacraments, community with one another, tradition and teaching of the wider Church and evangelisation.

### Who do people say the Son of Man is? Who do you say I am? (Matthew 16:13-19)

These questions help us to explore the centre of our faith, namely the person of Christ, and to see how far we always have to travel to accept him fully as Saviour for the world.

*'Our experience of Church begins with knowing Jesus Christ and learning to respond to him as disciples.'*

### The Wedding Feast at Cana (John 2:1-11)

This familiar story is not just about a wedding or about marriage but has huge implications for the whole Church and particularly for the parish community. We identify the 'six water jars' that are there to be filled by us as: Building Community; Ecumenism; Social issues of justice, peace and equality; Empowerment of the laity; Involvement of young people; Centrality of Marriage and Family Life.

### The Transfiguration (Matthew 17:1-8)

Inspired by this story, we look at the five senses of a parish community and consider how we have a responsibility to constantly attend to each of these in the name of Christ. These five are: a sense of personal dignity for everyone; a sense of wonder and gladness; a sense of freedom; a sense of the presence of Christ; a sense of purpose.

### The Prayer of Christ (John 17)

This very significant chapter from the Gospels should give us a real sense of peace and a great sense of purpose. Christ is among us, praying for us all the time. And his prayer is for our unity. We examine something of what this means and look at the three building blocks for unity: unity of mind; unity of heart; unity of affection.

### The Commissioning of the Disciples (Matthew 28:16-20)

With this passage we listen to the five commands Christ makes to his disciples and to us. Go; make disciples of all nations; baptise them in the name of the Father, and of the Son, and of the Holy Spirit; teach them to observe all the commands I gave you; know that I am with you always, yes to the end of time.

We hope you find inspiration from what follows.

## 17. THE DISCIPLES ON THE ROAD TO EMMAUS

*(Luke 24:13-35)*

This well-known story from St Luke's Gospel is very relevant for us in the Church today. It is a crisis story. The two disciples had been with Jesus. Everything seemed to be full of promise and suddenly with the crucifixion of Christ, everything now seemed to be shattered. They were giving up. Jesus walks with them and they receive new energy from a new way of perceiving him.

*'Service of others is at the heart of all our pastoral development, both in building up relationships within the local Church community and in reaching out to others wherever we find them.'*

*On the first day of the week, two of the disciples were on their way to a village called Emmaus, seven miles from Jerusalem, and they were talking together about all that had happened. Now as they talked this over, Jesus himself came up and walked by their side; but something prevented them from recognising him. He said to them, 'What matters are you discussing as you walk along?' They stopped short, their faces downcast.*

*Then one of them, called Cleopas, answered him, 'You must be the only person staying in Jerusalem who does not know the things that have been happening there these last few days.' 'What things?' he asked. 'All about Jesus of Nazareth,' they answered, 'who proved he was a great prophet by the things he said and did in the sight of God and of the whole people; and how our chief priests and our leaders handed him over to be sentenced to death, and had him crucified. Our own hope had been that he would be the one to set Israel free. And this is not all: two whole days have now gone by since it all happened: and some women from our group have astounded us; they went to the tomb in the early morning, and when they did not find the body, they came back to tell us they had seen a vision of angels who declared he was alive. Some of our friends went to the tomb and found everything exactly as the women had reported, but of him they saw nothing.'*

*Then he said to them, 'You foolish men! So slow to believe the full message of the prophets! Was it not ordained that the Christ should suffer and so enter into his glory?' Then, starting with Moses and going through all the prophets, he explained to them the passages throughout the scriptures that were about himself.*

*When they drew near to the village to which they were going, he made as if to go on; but they pressed him to stay with them. 'It is nearly evening,' they said, 'and the day is almost over.' So he went in to stay with them. Now while he was with them at table, he took the bread and said the blessing; then he broke it and handed it to them. And their eyes were opened and they recognised him; but he had vanished from their sight. Then they said to each other, 'Did not our hearts burn within us as he talked to us on the road and explained the scriptures to us?'*

*They set out that instant and returned to Jerusalem. There they found the eleven assembled together with their companions, who said to them, 'Yes, it is true. The Lord has risen and has appeared to Simon.' Then they told their story of what had happened on the road and how they had recognised him at the breaking of bread.*

## Parish Implications

### Restoring to hope

This is the story of disciples who had faith in Christ. They were talking together about him. And that's who we are; it is our story. It is also the story of disciples who loved Christ. They were talking about him with great affection and from broken hearts, now that he had been taken away from them. And that's who we are; it is our story. It is also our story in the fact that it is the story of disciples who had lost hope. Their whole world had collapsed through the events of Good Friday. Their lives were shattered. Not even the rumours of Christ having risen from the dead that were beginning to circulate could cheer them up. They were too afraid to hope again. Then Jesus walks with them and gently but firmly opens their eyes to see the deeper realities.

### What matters are you discussing as you walk along?

This is the question Jesus asks the two disciples and it is the question he asks us today: What matters are you discussing as you walk along? In the story from St Luke's Gospel, Cleopas answers: 'you must be the only one staying in Jerusalem who doesn't know the things that have been happening there these last few days.' He was speaking to the only one who did know but was so blinded by his own experience and expectations that he couldn't recognise Christ. He thought that what he saw was all there was to see, what he knew was all there was to know!

And that is most often our problem too. When we face the question of what we talk to each other about we will find that most of it is knocking the heart out of us. This is true whether we are talking about ourselves, or each other, or the Church, or the world around us. There is so much that is negative in all the aspects of life and we name it in reality. And we lose heart. Christ doesn't want us to ignore the negative realities but rather to put them in the context of his death and resurrection. In Christ everything has been redeemed, is being redeemed in the present and will be redeemed to the end of time. That is the deepest reality of human life. Our task is to keep making that reality possible and actual.

### Six elements of our spirituality

What happens in the rest of the story of the journey to Emmaus presents us with the six essential elements of spirituality for the disciples of Christ. These are: prayer, scripture, the Eucharist, community with one another, tradition of the Church and evangelisation. We take each of these six now and expand on them. But it is important to keep in mind that together they form the complete picture. In so far as one or other is weak or even missing, the full impact of Christ's salvation will not be recognised by us.

1.  Prayer
    The first purpose of prayer for the followers of Christ is to help them realise that Christ is always with them, among them, above them, below them, on their right side and on their left. Prayer is often used for purposes other than this. Prayer can be used as fulfilling a duty to God. It can be used to bargain with God or to threaten God. For us prayer needs to be constantly purified into becoming our way of rooting ourselves ever more fully in the presence of Christ so that we can grow in hope and in confidence in our mission to the world.

    The second purpose of prayer for us as Christ's followers is to equip us with all that we need to follow him. The two qualities mentioned above, namely hope and confidence, are essential. We need a lot of prayer to grow in those qualities. Other essential qualities of his followers are humility, by which we are at ease with our own limitations and those of others, and ready forgiveness, through which we can let go of the effects that these limitations impose on our spirits. We need to be able to forgive ourselves and each other so that we are not constantly rooted in the past through guilt or anger. As followers of Christ we need prayer to help us grow in appreciation of all the wonderful things of life and to become people of thanksgiving and praise towards God and each other. Prayer that helps us to know deeply the presence of Christ will ultimately lead us to the fulfilment of his two commandments as we become more and more a people who love God with our whole hearts, our whole minds, our whole strength and who love our neighbours as ourselves.

2.  Scripture

The second essential element of our spirituality is the Scriptures. When we come to the Scriptures, if we come to them at all, we so often try to discover what is in them. This is important for us because we have to study them in the context of different cultures and different times. But the Scriptures are given to us so that we can discover what is in us. Through the Scriptures, and only through them, we have revealed to us who we are – people made in the image and likeness of God; people who are so loved by God that God's own Son took human flesh to lead us back to God; people who are vital members of Christ's Body; people who have been given God's Holy Spirit to indwell with us; people who are filled with all the gifts of God's Spirit; people who have been given the mission to continue the saving work of Christ to the ends of the earth and to the end of time.

Through the Scriptures we also have revealed to us that we are sisters and brothers to all people and that everyone has a claim on our love. This is a very big way of living but settling for anything less is a betrayal of the will of God. Barriers that have constantly been built through the sinfulness of humanity need to be brought down. These barriers are built between men and women, between different nationalities and cultures, between different religions and between those who believe and those who don't. They are usually built to exercise control, to dominate, to protect interests. They can have no place in the lives of Christ's followers. He gave his ultimate command to us as: 'love your enemies; do good to those who harm you; pray for those who persecute you'.

Also through the Scriptures we have revealed to us the dignity of all creation and we are given the sacred task of caring for it in the name of God. In recent years environmentalists have reminded us very strongly of this sacred duty. Our following of Christ is not some nice, cosy religion where we can perform certain religious actions and feel self-satisfied. It is rather a taking on of the Spirit of God who looks at all creation and at humanity and declares loudly: 'it is very good'.

3. Eucharist

'They recognised him at the breaking of bread.' In our Catholic tradition the Eucharist is seen as 'the source and summit of our spirituality'. (Pope John Paul II). However, we continually reduce the real significance of the Eucharist to proportions that we can manage. For many Catholics it has become a burden imposed on them by law every Sunday. While many have rejected this 'burden' by giving up, many others continue to go with a lack of joy and expectation. This crippling reluctance is seen in how people talk about the length of Mass and often search out the quickest one. When we think like this we have clearly missed the point.

**A source of hope**

The Eucharist is one of the major ways Christ constantly restores his Church to hope. In it we gather the world into the death and resurrection of Christ and he redeems that world. In spite of the strong signs to the contrary, the world we live in is continuously being redeemed and sanctified in this way through the Eucharist we celebrate.

**A power of transformation**

In the Eucharist we are transformed. Pope John Paul II described every Eucharist as a time of conversion. The tradition of the Church clearly tells us that the Eucharist changes us into the Body of Christ. By eating the Body of Christ we become the Body of Christ. This tradition is very close to what nutritionists say today: we are what we eat. Through the Eucharist we are transformed from being mortal into immortal, finite into infinite, individuals into community. Of course we have to cooperate with this transformation and learn to live it gradually as we travel

through life. We certainly cannot let ourselves settle for Communion as some kind of nice private devotion.

## A missioning

One of the main reasons for the constant celebration of the Eucharist is that we may be sent out to our world with the Good News of Christ's salvation and of God's passionate love. The world that has been redeemed by Christ in our Eucharist has a right to know this Good News and so share in our hope. We do this, not by preaching to the world – although at times it is important for Christians to speak out clearly on subjects of justice and equality – but through the ways we live out the Eucharist we have celebrated. These ways are always new and fresh because in every Eucharist we are entrusted with a small portion of the Word of God to bring with us. We are also given particular qualities of life in each Eucharist through the prayers that are said at the beginning, after the Offertory and at the end of Communion. Because these have been prayed for we know they have been given. Our responsibility is to live them in the setting of our ordinary daily living.

4. ## Community with one another

Community with one another happens when we are together. However, we also need to build community so that whether we are together or apart we experience the support and love of one another. This building of community has to be deliberately worked at. We do this in a variety of ways. First of all, the official gatherings of the parish for Sunday Mass especially need to be made as good as possible for everyone. This can only happen when a parish is organised in such a way that there are people looking after and developing hospitality; when some people look out for the stranger and welcome her or him; when others take note of the recently bereaved or those with illness in the house and take care of these people; when others again can help parents with young children, or elderly people who may live alone and come to Mass alone. It can only be as good as possible when each one makes an effort to take a full part in the prayers of the liturgy and in the other parts of the Mass. In other words the gathering of the parish community for Sunday Mass will only be what it can and should be when we all take it on as our responsibility (not just the priest's) and contribute to

making it a real celebration of faith. The same is true of every other official gathering of the parish community.

We also work at building community by developing networks of friendship with one another. These friendships are vitally important for the health and well-being of the faith that we share. All of us have friendships from a variety of sources that serve many different needs. Friendship with people who share our faith and our values is also needed so that our faith can be supported and our values treasured. Some of those friendships should be within our own parish community.

And we work at building community by taking an active part in some of the groups that are serving the parish community in so many ways. A huge temptation is to leave all this to others either because we don't believe we have anything to bring, or because we are too busy with other things, or because we are afraid of involvement. Everyone has special gifts to bring to the community and it is only when we are putting those qualities at the service of others that the community will be built.

5. **Rooted in the tradition and teaching of the Church**
As soon as the disciples at Emmaus recognised the Lord, they immediately returned to the rest of the disciples to tell their story and have it confirmed by them. That is the process that always has to be followed so that we are protected from error. Each small community, whether it is a couple or family, a friendship community or an organisational one, must be placed at the service of the parish community. The parish in turn is part of the local Church of the diocese. And every diocese is united in faith, hope and love with and through our Holy Father, the Pope. This is not just an organisational image but rather one of a unity of persons where everyone has so much to bring and all of us have so much to receive.

### Importance of Tradition
The word 'tradition' conjures up the image of the way things have always been done. And people who hold this up as the ideal are generally only going on how things were always done in their own experience. What we mean by tradition here is the sense of particular things that we can trace and

find in the history of God's people. A good example of this is in the language of the Liturgy. Those whom we call traditionalists would often claim that Latin is the proper language for the Liturgy because it was always done like that. The vernacular language is a much more ancient tradition as indeed is the variety of expression that culture brings to the liturgy. Another good example is the highly clerical Church that we inherited. Many people think this is the way it should be just because that's how we have always known it. What we are developing today in the form of collaboration is a return to a much older way of being the Church.

In all of this, the value that true tradition holds up to us is that the particular shape should never become the issue for us. The only issue for the Church is the proclamation of Christ to the world. We take whatever shape is necessary for that to happen effectively.

*The only issue for the Church is the proclamation of Christ to the world.*

### A sense of history
Part of tradition is a sense of history. We badly need this today as we let ourselves become despondent about the state of the Church and the world. For over 2000 years the Church has not only survived worse times than we are experiencing but has come out of them stronger and healthier than ever. And that will be true for us today in so far as we engage and cooperate with the presence of Christ among us and the movement of the Spirit around us. We have nothing to fear except fear itself. We can live through the traumas of today with great confidence for the future.

### The importance of teaching
Our Catholic tradition has always deeply reverenced the teaching role of the Magisterium, the Bishops together with the Pope, in matters of faith and morals. This teaching power has been very necessary throughout the history of the Church when it was threatened by heresies of various kinds. It is also very necessary today as we face many complex questions that, because of the development of technology, have never had to be asked before.

However, adherence to the teaching of the Church should never simply make us 'yes' people. Teaching should raise more questions for us than answers. And it is the working

113

together on those questions that will help provide the answers. In the story of the Church a very important part of the teaching of answers came from what is called the *'sensus fidelium'*, the 'instinct of the faithful', which expresses itself in the general way most of the faithful choose to live their Christian faith. The *sensus fidelium* needs to be listened to today as always. A very good way of doing that listening is through Parish Pastoral Councils and all that goes with them.

The teaching authority of the Church should always help us to enter ever more fully into the mystery of Christ, the Son of God. And it should also help us to find the ways of best living in this mystery in our ordinary everyday lives. St Ignatius Loyola, the founder of the Jesuits, taught that our moral decisions are not just between good and evil but even more importantly between good and better. The teaching of the Church helps us to constantly reach towards the better and not settle for the mediocre.

## 6. Evangelisation

In the story of Emmaus, the two disciples invited the stranger to stay with them for the night because it was getting late and he would have been in danger if he moved on. They had not recognised the stranger as Jesus so they were taking a risk in having him stay with them. It was because of this generosity on their part that they eventually recognised him in the breaking of bread at their table. And then everything fell into place for them. They were able to say: 'Did not our hearts burn within us as he spoke to us on the road and explained the Scriptures to us?'

*That is what evangelisation is about: sharing what we have with the stranger.*

That is what evangelisation is about: sharing what we have with the stranger. Sometimes this sharing will be of our material possessions; sometimes it will be of our spiritual wealth. Whatever form it takes it carries with it a guarantee that we will always receive far more than we give, that we will always be enriched by generosity.

### Who are the strangers?

Many people today have become estranged from the life of the Church. We need to find the ways of opening up a dialogue with them to discover the reasons why they have left us, to ask for forgiveness from them where necessary and to

change our ways as we learn from them. Those who have left us may not know that a fresh spirit is beginning to blow through the Church and as a result they will be listened to and can make a difference.

Most countries now are becoming increasingly multicultural. As Christians we have a great responsibility to respond to this new situation in creative ways. We often have to tackle our innate racial prejudices in order to become a people of hospitality. As people from other cultures join our worshipping community we need to be open to change in order to accommodate them. And for those who need our help we need to be generous in providing for them. Our comfort zones are being challenged in new ways. And that is good for us.

Our young people today need us to take special care of them as they are in serious danger of losing a real knowledge of Christ as their saviour. Our schools are doing all they can to ensure that our young people can grow in faith. But our parish communities need to do a lot more to add to this. A lot of our attention and our resources need to go into claiming our young people for Christ. If we engage with this as a parish the benefits will be great as our young people will add a freshness to how we live and will provide a challenge to how we believe.

Conclusion
In spite of all the negative things that are happening among us and around us as the Church of today, we can dare to hope because we know that the power of Christ is at work among us and around us also. By developing these six elements of our spirituality we can become like the disciples in the early Church who were able to say: 'Yes it is true. The Lord has truly risen'.

# 18. THE PERSON OF CHRIST

*(Matthew 16:13-19)*

*'How do we need to be as a parish so that our children and young people growing up can have a living faith in Jesus Christ?'*

One of the important features of the Gospels is the questions Jesus asks his disciples. They are always questions that lead to growth of their understanding of him and of the nature of the Church. In this passage from St Matthew's Gospel there are two of these important questions: **Who do people say the Son of Man is? Who do you say I am?**

*When Jesus came to the region of Caesarea Philippi he put this question to his disciples, 'Who do people say the Son of Man is?' And they said, 'Some say he is John the Baptist, some Elijah, and others Jeremiah or one of the prophets'. 'But you,' he said, 'who do you say I am?' Then Simon Peter spoke up, 'You are the Christ,' he said, 'the Son of the living God'. Jesus replied, 'Simon son of Jonah, you are a happy man! Because it was not flesh and blood that revealed this to you but my Father in heaven. So I now say to you: You are Peter and on this rock I will build my Church. And the gates of the underworld can never hold out against it. I will give you the keys of the kingdom of heaven: whatever you bind on earth shall be considered bound in heaven; whatever you loose on earth shall be considered loosed in heaven.'*

## Parish Implications

### Who do people say the Son of Man is?

This doesn't seem like a very relevant question for us today. It is a question that comes from an obviously religious context and we can say that our situation generally is not very religious! However, this question is as relevant now as ever but we have to look at it from a particular angle. Every human person is looking for something better than what they have. So we could rephrase this question from St Matthew's Gospel and phrase it in a number of ways: Where do people look for their hope? Where do people look for their happiness? Where do people today look for their future? When we ask those questions we can see that people look in all sorts of places and towards all kinds of people.

There are a few recognised sources of hope for people in our society. They are very important elements in human life but they can also be full of false promise.

## Possessions

Our society puts great emphasis on riches as a sign of human success. And of course it is important that people get on as well as possible. But when it becomes the purpose of life, as it does for so many people, then it becomes divisive of human community. So much energy is put into getting more and more for ourselves that we often don't have time and space for the really important things of life. Our society has developed the 'Lotto' mentality where countless numbers of people do the Lotto twice a week in the hope of hitting the jackpot. And week after week those same people are disappointed but there is always the next week to keep them hoping. The implication is that if we could only get wealthy enough then we would be happy; we would be saved. And the experience of life teaches us that this is not necessarily true because the more we have the more we have to protect and we can become the prisoners of our own possessions. Possessions possess us. And we can easily cross over to seeing those who don't have anything as non-persons, or even as enemies of our status.

## Position and power

A second source of hope for people today is that of getting to 'the top of the ladder', whatever particular direction their life is going in. Of course, this need touches on a very important aspect of human life, namely our desire to be recognised and valued. So much human energy is spent on getting a better job, a promotion, being in charge of more people. And people's dignity gets associated with the dignity of the job or profession a person has. This mentality has a serious effect on our education services which are largely shaped by the points-system so that the more points you get, the better job you will get, and the more respected you will become in society. The first obvious defect of this mentality is the implication that those who don't get the high points, the big job, are less in terms of human dignity. They feel this themselves and our systems continue to reinforce this. And countless people are alienated within themselves and from taking a full part in the formation of human society.

Even for those who do succeed in getting to the top of the very many ladders of life, this mentality has so many pitfalls. First of all, success does not necessarily bring happiness. In fact the effort to get there can often bring ulcers or can result in a nervous condition that has to be constantly boosted by alcohol or medication or drugs of various kinds. How often we hear of people who live in the fast lane ending up as human wrecks.

Secondly, by the time a person gets to the top of the ladder, it is near time to come back down again! And there will always be plenty of people to help in the descent! And then comes retirement which so often brings with it a sense of emptiness. This is especially true for those who have become dependent on their particular job or profession or position for their sense of worth in their own eyes or in the eyes of others. In retirement they have nothing to live for, they have little or no sense of purpose for their lives.

Obviously, it is important that every person have the fullest possible opportunity of success in life. But when this becomes the purpose of human life and the sign of a real human being, then it is seriously flawed and urgently needs to be reviewed and redirected.

**Pleasure**

In the search for human fulfilment, a third direction is very often pursued, namely that of pleasure. The mentality here is 'if I can enjoy myself all the time, then I will be happy.' Pleasure in human life is essential and we have a right to expect to enjoy living. However, when it becomes the reason for living we are going to become greatly disappointed and disillusioned. Of course, the Church, and religion in general, has a lot to repent of in regard to this need for and right to enjoy the pleasures of life. In the Catholic experience one of the frequent questions in the Sacrament of Confession used to be, 'Did you take pleasure in it?' The implication was that if you did, then whatever it was you were talking about was almost certainly seriously sinful! If you didn't take pleasure in it, then it was probably sinful anyway but maybe not as serious! This mentality continues to show through in any place where we find fundamentalism in faith or in religion.

As was stated earlier, we have a right to enjoy our human living. But there are also other vital elements in human life that have to be respected and lived through like pain, suffering, self-sacrifice, self-denial and putting others first. The culture that is developing around us today tends to exclude these realities as much as possible and many people, especially our young people, become disappointed with and despondent about their own experiences. What is held up to our young people as the ultimate in life is an endless round of parties and gigs in which the pleasures of life are all available on demand. And yet the incidence of suicide is growing at an alarming pace among our young people. How do we face this apparent contradiction today? It all depends on how we manage the delicate balance between our rights and responsibilities and build a confidence in ourselves to cater adequately for both.

## Who do you say I am?

It is into this reality of the human struggle for happiness that Jesus places his second question to his disciples: 'Who do you say I am?' Peter answers this question immediately: 'You are the Christ, the Son of the living God.' And Jesus replies: 'And you are Peter, and on this rock I will build my Church, and the gates of the underworld can never hold out against it.' This dialogue between Jesus and Peter is a very significant one for our whole understanding of our life of faith.

Peter's act of faith: 'You are the Christ, the Son of the living God', is basically saying that Christ is the only one who can teach us God, and teach us human living. He is our only saviour, our only source of hope, and his way is the only way to full human living. And when Jesus says to Peter: 'On this rock I will build my Church', he is not just talking about the person of Peter but rather about the statement of faith that Peter has just made. That statement is the core statement of our Christian faith, that Christ is our way, our truth and our life.

## Simple but not easy

In practice, the Church has struggled with fully accepting Christ right from the very beginning. We see this in their answers to his first question: 'Who do people say the Son of Man is?' They answered: 'Some say he is John the Baptist, some Elijah, others Jeremiah or one of the prophets'.

In the early Church there were people who would have preferred if John the Baptist was the Messiah. Several times in the Gospels we find John pushing people away from him saying things like: 'No! I am not the one. There is one coming after me. He is the one.' And the people would seem to be saying things like: 'but we want you.' John the Baptist was more like what they were looking for – someone who told it as it was, calling for repentance and for people to face up to their sinfulness. We still have that syndrome in the Church today, what I call the John the Baptist syndrome. It is seen where people stand in judgement on the world and long for someone to come and sort it out. The trouble is that it is always others who need sorting out rather than those who are looking for this sorting out to happen! Jesus calls on us to sort ourselves out and then the world will be a much better place!

In the early Church many people also remained rooted in the Old Testament either in terms of the Prophets or the Law. Some had their own favourite prophets like Elijah or Jeremiah, and everything about Jesus was examined in the light of that particular prophet. We are in danger of that same difficulty, where other people or other events take precedence over our full listening to the teaching of Jesus. As Catholics we are in the middle of that struggle at present, where the strength of the Church became our reason for confidence. Now that the position of the Church is greatly reduced in society and the respect for the Church is greatly diminished through the revelations of the sinfulness of its members, many people find it impossible to believe. The structures, the position, the power of the Church can easily become what we are looking for and Jesus is then fitted into that.

We also see this mentality expressed in the way so many people respond today to private revelations and their public expression in places like Medjugorje and Fatima and in events like the film *The Passion of the Christ*. These places are all very important places of pilgrimage and should be encouraged. But we also have to be very mindful of how they can so easily take over from the Scriptures, the Tradition of the Church and the Word of God that is speaking to us from all of creation. Some advocates of these places would seem almost to take delight in passing on revelations of negative judgement on the world we live in and depend on the creation of fear as our motivation for changing our lives. The place or the people of the revelations become our focus and the Good News of Christ tends to be fitted into those and God's love and Christ's salvation once again become conditional.

In the early Church many people also remained rooted in the Old Testament through their focus on the Law as the way we are to be saved. The Church is always under severe pressure to go in that direction. Of course the Law is of extreme importance and calls for our deepest reverence. This holds true for the law as found in the Old Testament, especially the Ten Commandments. It holds true also for the many laws that govern our Church today through which we develop a discipline of worship and of right living. But the law, no matter how important or good it is, cannot save us. Our faith is firmly rooted in the knowledge that Christ is our only Saviour. The task of the church is to constantly return to that truth and to promote full acceptance of Christ in the minds and hearts and lives of all her members.

How do we know when we personally and as a Church have fully accepted Christ as the Son of the living God?

There are four main tests through which we can know how fully we have accepted Christ.

1.  **How we think about and relate to God**

    **A Distant God**
    The Church is not always faithful to the God of Jesus Christ. In the past, and maybe even to some extent in the present, God is presented as someone who is far removed from us in time and space. In an effort to acknowledge the transcendence of God we made God distant from us. A result of this has been that Catholic spirituality became a spirituality of preparing for death. The implication here was often that this is the moment when the individual was going to meet God. It was thought of as a dreadful moment. But each one could be prepared for it. Of course death is a very special happening in the life of every human person, and we should be as prepared as possible for it. But dread of meeting God should have no place in this.

    **A Punishing God**
    Another aspect of this in our Catholic spirituality has been thinking of God as our Judge. The way this is often presented is not just a Judge but a harsh Judge. How many people have grown up with 'don't do that, God is watching' ringing in their ears. And it was only what we were doing

wrong that God seemed to be watching! The image that many people developed for themselves was of this distant God, noting all the sins of people and when they died God would hammer hell out of them! This is not the God of Jesus Christ.

## A Manipulating God

Another common concept of God in people's spirituality is of God pulling the strings in everyone's life. This can be seen when there is a disaster in someone's life, for instance, when someone dies suddenly, or there is an accident or an earthquake. The most common question at those times is 'Why did God do that?' or 'If God is so good how could this be allowed to happen to me?' The implication here is that God is controlling all these events directly and deciding on everything that happens, especially all the negative things that happen in our lives. This also is not the God that Jesus reveals to us.

## The God of Jesus

(a) In acknowledging Christ as the Son of God, we are accepting that only he can teach us what God is like. And he teaches us what God is like in relationship to ourselves. In his own humanity, Christ teaches us that, far from being distant from us, God has come very close to us. He was able to say words like: 'Whatever you do to even the least of my brothers or sisters you do to me'. We are meeting God every day in all our human dealings, even with those we think of as least deserving of our attention. And our judgement is taking place every day in those circumstances of human life – 'I was hungry and you gave me food to eat', 'I was hungry and you refused to give me food to eat.'

Or again Jesus tells us: 'Where two or three are gathered together in my name I am there with them'. As baptised people we are always gathered in Christ's name whatever the reason for our being together. We are always walking on holy ground because God in Christ is always among us.

(b) In his person Christ teaches us how close God has come to us. In his words he teaches us what God is like. This is especially true when he tells us to think of God as our Father. In the Scriptures God is also thought of as our

*We are always walking on holy ground because God in Christ is always among us.*

Mother. Our human minds and our language are very limited. A sign of this is that we can only think male and female and we have been taught to think of God almost exclusively as male. This of course is rightly being challenged today. And yet we have to be able to find language that completely reverences Christ's revelation of the deep personal love that God has for each one of us. This is best seen in the individual love that a mother or father has for her/his children.

There are some special characteristics of this parental love that are true of God's love for each one individually.

**(i)** The first of these is that parents always carry each of their children with them in their minds and hearts. Even when parents get away for a night or a weekend or a holiday, the first thing they generally do is to phone home to make sure everyone is alright. In calling God Father/Mother, Jesus is telling us that this is how God is with us. We are never out of God's thoughts; we are never far from God's heart. And this is true whether we are good or bad, whether we are living according to God's way or not. There are no conditions set for God's love for us.

**(ii)** The second great quality that parents so often exhibit is their generous commitment to and investment of themselves in the well-being of their children. And that is how God is with us. Far from 'being away in heaven', God has shown how much we mean by giving us Jesus who suffered and died so that we might know and believe. The revolution of the Christian revelation is that God adores us.

**(iii)** A third reality about parents is that they cannot lead their children's lives for them. No matter how much they give to each one in their family, no matter how much love and affection they shower on them, ultimately each person has to live her/his life and take responsibility for it. God is like that with us. This is what we mean by free will because God will not force us to live in a particular way. However, just as parents generally do not disown a daughter or son no matter how they turn out, so too God will never disown us but will always wait and hope and pray that we will come back to know how fully we are forgiven and how totally we are loved.

(c) Through his Spirit Christ teaches us what God is like in relation to each of us. The Scripture talks about God as Love. 'God is love and those who live in love live in God and God in them.' (1 Jn 4:16). The Scripture also talks about God as compassion, with a full understanding heart; as forgiveness that is constantly given long before we ask.

### The Difficulty of letting go

In many ways, it is easier on us to look at God as distant from our lives. Then we can develop a religion that keeps God happy with us because we fulfil our duties. We then reduce these to a minimum. As Catholics, we have done this by identifying the practice of faith with going to Mass on Sunday.

It is even easier to look on God as judge, as one who is going to punish us. We can control this God to a good extent by our good behaviour so that God won't have too much against us.

With the God of Jesus however we have no control at all. He reveals God as one who loves us with an extreme love. Instead of being all powerful God has become all weakness because of love for each of us. It is awesome just to think of this. It is also scary to think of the consequences of this, particularly that this love of God is held back from no one, not even those whom we would condemn, those we would write off, those we would despise. Every human heart has the right to hear the word of God spoken into it: 'I love you, you are mine.' 'I have carved you on the palm of my hand.' That will only happen if and when we as the Church fully accept Christ and let go to his word and his way.

2.  How we think about and relate to ourselves

    As Catholics we don't have a very good history of self-love. How many people got out of bed this morning, looked in the mirror and said: 'You are beautiful, you are wonderful, I love you'? We would be more inclined to look in the mirror and criticise ourselves and express some sort of self-loathing. That is not the way of Christ.

Our spirituality has often been one of this kind of self-loathing. It was promoted in the name of humility and forms of discipline were developed in family life and in religious life to ensure that we knew we were no good. What people called humility was more often humiliation and did untold damage to countless people.

Every person has a right to know how good she/he is. We have all got a right to be proud of ourselves because there is so much goodness and beauty in every human person. Our systems and disciplines need to be geared towards this self-love and self-approval if we are to take Christ seriously.

The very beginning of the Scriptures reveals to us that we are created in the image and likeness of God. That is our basic nature, a nature that has been marred by sin but has not been changed or destroyed by sin. If we are made in God's image we cannot in any way play down the beauty and goodness of ourselves.

The Scripture also tells us that our bodies are temples of God's Holy Spirit. What a wonderful revelation that is and what an extraordinary grace. But how do we deal with it? So often our spirituality has made us suspicious of our bodies, sometimes even to the point of despising ourselves and considering that as virtue. If it is true, and as Christians we believe it to be so, that our bodies are temples of God's Spirit, then we need to develop a spirituality of a healthy respect for our bodies and a holy freedom in relation to our human nature.

We are filled with the gifts of creation and the further gifts of the Spirit. Unfortunately we are all conditioned to think of ourselves as important and as good only in terms of success. We are always in competition with others in our minds and hearts and we put ourselves down because others are more important because they are wealthier, more famous, better looking, younger, more popular and so on. All of this has no place in our following of Christ and our acceptance of him as our saviour. He teaches us to be glad of who we are, to rejoice in our own goodness, to love ourselves. True humility is to be found then in acknowledging that all this goodness and beauty and wonder are gifts from God. And our lives are lived in an awesome worship of this God who is so good to us and who loves us with a passionate love.

3.  **How we think about and relate to other people**

    In practice most of us are so busy living our own lives that
    other people in general don't take up much of our time or
    attention. Of course there are a few people who are our
    family or friends and these we love. There may be a few
    others who are our enemies and these we deal with in various
    ways. But people in general don't impinge on our daily
    living.

    Christ changes all that for us if we accept him fully into our
    lives. He reveals to us that every person is our sister or
    brother. And every person has a right to our love and our
    care. Christianity is a very big way of living because the
    Christian heart expands to the ends of the earth. We can see
    this in practice in so many of the Saints who gave their lives
    for others because they felt the hunger or the pain or the
    loneliness or the desperation of people in the world. But we
    see it also lived out in the lives of many very ordinary people
    in our parishes. These are the people who respond to the
    needs of their neighbours and also to the needs of the world.
    When there is a disaster of some kind, a famine or an
    earthquake, they immediately respond because they feel for
    those in need. They may never meet them but they already
    have them in their hearts. That is the call to each of us who
    call ourselves Christians. Sometimes we hear people talking
    about some person as a good Christian 'because she/he
    would not do anyone any harm'. That is not what
    Christianity is about. That is ordinary human decency and is
    to be admired and encouraged. Christianity is about
    positively doing good to every person and not just not doing
    them any harm. Christianity is not just about 'not saying a
    bad word about anybody'. It is about saying a good word
    about everybody. It is about building up the quality of life for
    those in need. It is about taking responsibility for those
    around us and those who are far away.

    The ultimate commandment Christ gives us is: 'Love your
    enemies. Do good to those who harm you. Pray for those
    who persecute you'. It seems almost impossible. It certainly
    seems a lot of the time to be undesirable and almost foolish.
    Yet Christ doesn't put any 'ifs' or 'buts' into his word. Ours
    is no small, insignificant religion that can be practised by
    fulfilling a few religious duties. Ours is a big, vibrant way of

life that is full of challenge and full of possibilities because it promises freedom to live life to the full.

4.  ## How we think about and relate to the world we live in
    Our spirituality at times has taught us to be suspicious of the world we live in. Religious life was seen at times as 'getting away from the world' in order to live a holy life. We identified the three sources of human downfall as: 'the world, the flesh, and the devil'. Of course there is wisdom in these attitudes and there is also a good sense of facing up to reality. There is no doubt that the world is full of all kinds of evil. It is a major source of temptation away from God. But that is not by any means the full truth of the world because it is also full of goodness and beauty and the wonder of God. Far from 'getting away from the world' the Christian develops holiness by becoming immersed in the world and revealing there the Kingdom of God.

    ### The world of nature/creation
    In the Book of Genesis the word of God tells us the beautiful story of the creation of the world. It's not about believing the details of this story but catching the spirit of it that forms our faith. Everything that exists comes from God and has its being because of God. The implication is obvious. Everything in nature is sacred because God can be found there. Humanity is seen as the climax of this creative action of God. And humanity is also seen as the greatest enemy to its fulfilment. Original sin didn't just affect humanity but had a serious effect on all of nature which is now groaning for salvation. Humanity continues to be the greatest enemy to our world as men and women farm nature not just for survival and growth but for blatant greed.

    As Christians we have a serious responsibility to reverence this world of nature, to farm it in ways that will lead to its enhancement and to vigorously oppose any and all attempts to destroy it. We need to be people of the earth and people of the universe. We need to call all humanity to give glory to God by how we treat this wonderful gift of our world.

    ### The world of humanity
    As we listen to and watch the news day by day we could very easily get despondent. There seems to be so much violence

and destruction in our world. People are becoming more afraid of life and of what the future holds and no one seems to be able to do anything about it.

In the Gospels there is a lovely scene of Jesus among his disciples looking at the crowds around them and proclaiming: 'the harvest is great'. That continues to be the only proper Christian response to the world around us today. In spite of all the evil in our world, and all the inhuman actions of person to person, there is a great potential for good. As Christians we have a responsibility to work for that potential and build it up for the unity of our human family to the glory of God. We don't ever have to save the world. We cannot do that anyhow! But we have to work to make it possible for Christ to save the world and complete the Kingdom of God.

*In spite of all the evil in our world, and all the inhuman actions of person to person, there is a great potential for good.*

We do this by working for peace in our own surroundings as well as in the world. We do it by calling for justice for all people, especially for those who are powerless and voiceless and vulnerable. We live out our faith for the good of humanity by being full time promoters of equality between women and men; young and old, rich and poor, all religions and none.

And we help to bring humanity into the salvation of Christ by being in the forefront for the dignity of every human person from conception to natural death. We believe that that dignity continues beyond death into eternal life. The dignity of the saints is not a new one that is granted in heaven. It is the same dignity and reverence that every human person has a right to at every stage of their journey through life.

Jesus proclaimed: 'The harvest is great'. Then he added: 'but the labourers are few.' This is not just about vocations to religious life and priesthood. Rather it is about recognising the enormity of the task we have and the wonder of that task. And then each of us takes our own place fully in accomplishing that task, the transformation of our world.

# 19. THE WEDDING FEAST AT CANA

## *John 2, 1-11*

The scene of this story in St John's Gospel is a wedding. There is a significance in that of course. But it is not about marriage so much as about the Church. This story brings us into the deepest reality of the Church, namely Jesus among his disciples transforming the world around them.

*On the third day there was a wedding at Cana in Galilee. The mother of Jesus was there and Jesus and his disciples had also been invited. When they ran out of wine, since the wine provided for the wedding was all finished, the mother of Jesus said to him, 'They have no wine'. Jesus said, 'Woman, why turn to me? My hour has not come yet.' His mother said to the servants, 'Do whatever he tells you'. There were six stone water jars standing there, meant for the ablutions that are customary among the Jews; each could hold twenty or thirty gallons. Jesus said to the servants, 'Fill the jars with water', and they filled them to the brim. 'Draw some out now' he told them 'and take it to the steward.' They did this; the steward tasted the water and it had turned into wine. Having no idea where it came from – only the servants who had drawn the water knew – the steward called the bridegroom and said, 'People generally serve the best wine first, and keep the cheaper sort till the guests have had plenty to drink; but you have kept the best wine till now'.*

*This was the first of the signs given by Jesus; it was given at Cana in Galilee. He let his glory be seen, and his disciples believed in him. After this he went down to Capernaum with his mother and his brothers and sisters, but they stayed there only a few days.*

## Parish Implications

The greatest temptation of the Church is to put other things, other people, at the centre and inevitably things fall apart. We can be tempted to think that if we get everything properly organised and everyone brought into line, we will be saved. It doesn't work. If people can only be brought to keep the law then everything will be all right. It doesn't work. We can tend to put particular movements or significant private revelations or special practices at the centre and try to bring everyone into conformity with these. It doesn't work.

The greatest task of the Church in every generation is to keep restoring Christ to the centre and, by listening to his word with open lives, attend to the world we live in. This is the only way to be the Church today as in every generation.

Our Catholic tradition strongly reflects the second important element of the Church that is found in the story of Cana, namely that Mary is very close to the centre. It is through her dialogue with her Son and with the people around them that the miracle of transformation is set up. She speaks the needs of the people to Jesus – 'they have no wine' – and she gives her one and only command to the servants – 'do whatever he tells you'. This on-going interaction is a very important part of our understanding of our spirituality.

*'Just as the parish priest has to make a conscious decision to work with others in partnership, the pastoral council has to decide consciously and deliberately to create an ever-extending network of partnerships, inviting people to become involved in developing the life of the parish, and empowering them to take on responsibility and to share it in their turn.'*

In the Gospel story of Cana, Mary gave her command to the servants: 'Do whatever he tells you'. And Jesus told them: 'Fill the water jars with water'. In the circumstances this must have seemed ridiculous. They had just run out of wine at the wedding feast. The last thing that was needed was 120 gallons of water! But the servants did it. And, as the Gospel story tells us: 'They filled them to the brim'. This probably wasn't done with any grace or good humour but rather in anger. But it was at this point that the miracle took place. The water had turned into wine. And they had a wedding feast that is still remembered and talked about more than two thousand years later!

'Do whatever he tells you.' That is still Mary's only command to the Church. How do we know what Jesus is telling us today in our generation? There are three sources of his word to us and it is only through listening to the three together that we get a full picture of his call to us.

1. The Scriptures: We refer to the Scriptures as the Word of God and so they are. We believe that the Scriptures are divinely inspired and give us a clear vision of what God wants for all creation and for each one of us.

2. The teaching and tradition of the Church: Throughout the centuries the Church has interpreted and applied the Scriptures to human life and to the world of every generation. We believe that the word of God comes to us through this action of interpretation and we need to listen keenly to it.

3.  The world in which we live: God, in Christ, is present in the
    Scriptures and in the teaching and tradition of the Church
    but he is in no way confined to these. He is also present in
    the people of the Church and expresses himself in what is
    called the 'sensus fidelium', the way people of the Church
    generally think and act. And God, in Christ, is present in
    every human person and every human situation and in all of
    his creation. We need also to listen intently to what is called
    the 'signs of the times' and learn appropriate ways of
    responding in his name.

All these sources of God's word have to be listened to together.
We can easily listen to one or other source while neglecting the
others and we end up in a cul-de-sac. For example, as Catholics,
we tended to concentrate almost exclusively on the teaching and
tradition of the Church for our knowledge of God's word. There
are historic reasons of being under siege for this concentration
but the results were that we lost, to a good extent, our contact
with the Scriptures. We also lost touch, again not entirely but to
a good extent, with the call of God in the struggles of human life
and built a fortress of possessing the truth. We are reclaiming the
Scriptures thankfully and we are once more opening up to
respond to the realities of life.

Other Christian Churches put their dependence totally on the
Scriptures. To a great extent they lost touch with the teaching
and interpreting power of the Church leadership. Private
interpretation became a way of faith for many of them with all
the consequent pitfalls this brings. Many of these Christian
Churches are relearning and reclaiming the importance of
teaching and tradition, and are responding to the changing needs
of the world with more focus.

Many people today want to be Christian but without the Church.
Very often this is in response to how they see the Church as
irrelevant to the world we live in. They pursue many important
social issues and render great service to humanity. But without
the Scriptures, which are rooted in the faith community, and
without the tradition and teaching that emanates from the
community of faith, these social issues can become crusades or
personal possessions and lose a lot of their possibilities for real
transformation.

So, how can we determine what Christ is calling us to today? The Second Vatican Council in the 1960s listened deeply to all three sources of God's Word and produced for us a vitally important response that would have far-reaching implications for every part and level of the Church. In a way, what this historic Council and consequent developments showed was that there are six 'water jars' standing there to be filled by us that will lead to the renewal of the Church and to the transformation of the world. We have to learn from the servants at Cana and 'fill them to the brim'.

1. **Building Community**

   This is the first and primary task of the Church at every level. It is a very central concept in the Scriptures, in both Old and New Testaments. God called 'a people' to himself, the Chosen People. Christ gathered his apostles and disciples around him as the beginning of the new people of God. The tradition of the Church, as gathered together in the teaching of the Second Vatican Council has, as a very central tenet, that we are a people, a pilgrim people, the people of God. And the world we live in today is calling for us to be a community so that hope can be brought to an increasingly divided and individualistic society.

   Building community has to be a very deliberate movement. In undertaking it we are fighting the tendency towards private spirituality. And we are also fighting the current strong trend towards individualism. Building community has constantly to avoid the tendency to become exclusive and comfortable. The community of faith always opens outwards to ensure there is a place for everyone who wants a home among us.

   Our efforts at building community with one another as Catholics go in two directions. Firstly, these efforts come from our identification with one another through our communion with our Holy Father the Pope. This is made more specific through the local Church of the diocese and is lived out in our parish community. And it is there in the parish community that our efforts have to be most evident, drawing us into community in ways that form an ever stronger link with the other parishes in the diocese, throughout the region, country, around the world and back into that place where Our Holy Father calls us to follow Christ.

## 2. Ecumenism

The second major task for the Church today is to strenuously work towards unity of the Christian Churches at every level. Many Catholics would see this as optional for them and would have little or no interest in Ecumenism. Yet it is a part of the practice of our faith.

We hear this call to unity in the Scriptures, most especially in the wonderful chapter 17 of St. John's Gospel, the continuous prayer of Jesus for the Church. It is prayer for total unity. The Second Vatican Council committed us to this direction to such a degree that this commitment is now enshrined in our Code of Canon Law. And certainly the world we live in demands that we work seriously at healing the hurts and mending the divisions between us if Christ is to be believable to people today.

This work towards unity has to be done at every level of the Church's life. A lot of very good work is being accomplished by theologians who are sifting through the differences in belief and looking for all our common ground – and there is a lot of it. Good work is also being done by our Holy Father and by bishops and other leaders of the Churches as they meet and pray together in a search for common directions in the world of today. The work of Ecumenism must also reach into every local parish and community where the hurts of the past and present are most acutely felt and where healing needs to be even more acutely applied. This involves getting to know each other; generously asking forgiveness and granting this forgiveness in Christ's name; finding opportunities to pray together, to socialise together, to normalise relationships. All of this is not easy but it has to be engaged with. There are many prejudices to be let go of; there are vested interests to be recognised and surrendered; there is apathy to be overcome. But there can be no doubt that it is a direction we must move in if we are to be faithful to Christ and his Gospel.

And as we move closer into unity with our Christian sisters and brothers, we are also called into relationship with the peoples of other world religions and none. The days when we Catholics claimed to have all the truth and everyone else was in error have to be really and truly gone. The new era, when we can confidently bring our truth and our uncertainty and place them alongside the truth and the uncertainties of other human beings, is now dawning. And it stretches us beyond ourselves.

3.  **Social Issues**

    The focus of the Church has to be the transformation of the world in which we live so that we can claim it for the Kingdom of God. It is so easy to get caught into internal affairs either within our own Catholic community or in our efforts to build unity with the other Christian Churches. When we do this, so much of our energy gets spent on concerns that have nothing to do with this transformation of the world. Then we become largely irrelevant and as such are acceptable to society. In his prayer at the Last Supper Jesus prayed: 'may they be so completely one that the world may believe that it was you who sent me' (Jn 17). The very purpose of our unity, our strength, our hope, our faith, is to bring the world we live in into the Kingdom of God.

    **Human dignity**

    A primary principle of God's Kingdom is the dignity of every human person made in the image and likeness of God. Because of this we, as Christians, need to be known as a people who uphold that dignity from conception until death and beyond. In our world there are many forces that threaten and oppose this sacred dignity of the human person. The abortion society threatens it in the mother's womb, where the foetus is seen as less than human, with no rights, and can be done away with.

    The consumerist society sees the human person as valuable only in so far as she/he is useful for production. We see this mentality in how more and more parents are putting their babies and young children into crèches to be reared by strangers so that they are free to work outside the home. Another result of this is the proliferation of nursing homes where our elderly people have to spend their declining years because no one has the time or the desire to care for them at home. Both these scenarios are so common now that they seem normal, and to question their effect on human dignity is an unpopular exercise and to be rendered a useless exercise as quickly as possible. The criminal society sees the human

*A primary principle of God's Kingdom is the dignity of every human person made in the image and likeness of God.*

person as expendable and human life as cheap. This mentality can so easily cross over to those who don't see themselves as criminals but whose behaviour can be modelled on the mentality that the only sin is getting caught.

## Equality of esteem

Another very important value of the kingdom of God is the equality of esteem that every human person deserves. Every person is created in the image and likeness of God and as such is due the greatest respect. And yet we live in a world that is very far from this ideal. There are all kinds of inequalities between people and all of us have our prejudices. The inequalities need to be tackled by us as a community that follows the wonderful social teaching of the Catholic Church; our prejudices need to be tackled by each of us individually.

There is a scandalous inequality between nations on a global level. In the West we have wealth that we don't know what to do with. And in other parts of the world people are starving to death on a daily basis. Within each country of the world there is a divide between rich and poor where the rich own a disproportionate amount of the wealth and use it to accrue more while there are homeless people often living on their doorstep. These various inequalities, which have always been with us and probably always will be, are the places for the prophetic voice of Christians to be heard. But that voice cannot dare speak if the same inequalities are in existence within our community. And unfortunately they often are.

Our prejudices also have to be a matter of great concern for us in our following of Christ. These can include colour and race in the Ireland of today; sexism; ageism; different religions or different forms of Christianity; sexual orientation; people we judge as not living life properly; etc. And we either write others off for these or similar reasons or we don't have anything to do with them and we just live our lives as if they were not there. The command of Jesus is universal, to love our neighbour as ourselves and to love our enemies, to do good to those who harm us, to pray for those who persecute us. It is no easy way but it is possible and we need the support from one another to keep working at it.

### Peace I leave with you

A third principle of God's kingdom is peace. It was one of the last gifts that Christ gave to his followers. And yet we live in a world that is so distant from this longing of his and this gift. It is a world where war is a daily reality, where violence is rife, where people live in dread in so many parts of our world. We ourselves have a society that is increasingly marked with stories of horrific murders, domestic violence, child abuse, abortion, etc. Of course there are very many good things about our world and our society and our homes. But the human heart is constantly coarsened by sin and selfishness. The task of the Church is to even more constantly claim the human heart for God. We need to be in the forefront of efforts that are aimed at building peace in our world. Of course there are many agendas involved in peace efforts. For us as the Church, the only acceptable agenda is the will of God. That takes a lot of purification of our own ways of seeing things so that we can see through his eyes.

4. **Empowerment of the laity**

   All the above cannot be accomplished unless there is a fundamental shift of emphasis in the Church from an ordained focus to a baptised focus. There is no doubt that the priesthood is a vitally important part of the life of the Church and of our whole Catholic tradition. However, over the generations more and more things have become associated with the ordained priest that, if there were enough priests, there would be very little need for anyone else except as receivers. That is now seen as an unhealthy way to live as Church. In ways we are being forced into seeing things differently because of the shortage of priests. We have still to travel the road to recognising that this new way is the right way in itself. Empowerment of the laity does not mean sharing some of the power of the priest with lay people so that things can more or less go on as before. It is about setting free the power that has been given to each person in her/his baptism and confirmation for the building up of the Church and for the evangelisation of the world. This takes a lot of discernment, much patience, an openness to making mistakes and correcting them, a letting go of fear and competition and trusting one another in faith.

### For the internal life of the Church

The laity of the Church have a very important part to play in the development of the internal life of the Church in terms of spirituality and worship. The two ways in which we are most familiar with this in practice concern Ministers of the Word and Eucharistic Ministers. Both of these forms of lay ministry are very widely accepted and are a good development in our Catholic practice. But we can be tempted to stop there and think that this is all it is about. Some of our parishes are pushing this out a little bit further into forms of Eucharistic Services that are conducted by lay people. Many other parishes resist this as a step too far. And yet we will be forced there and far beyond as the shortage of priests continues to grow and we will move ahead with regret rather than with gladness. There are many rituals and blessings that many lay people could do better than many priests because of the particular gifts they have especially among our women. But all of these continue to be tied into ordained ministry. Should they be? Beyond that again there is the world of lay participation in the other sacraments of the Church such as reconciliation, anointing of the sick, baptism. Everything of any significance in the celebration of these sacraments remains in the hands of the priest and can only happen according to his availability. We have a long way to go in our investigation of this.

We have an equally long way to go in our recognition of the place of laity in the decision-making processes within the Church. We continue to have most of the decisions that affect people's lives of faith made by bishops and priests. There is a greater openness to listening to what people have to say but ultimately the decisions are made at the top. This can only change when it begins to take a different shape in parish life through a good model of Pastoral Councils in which laity and priests work together as partners in the decisions that are necessary for the health and well-being of the community. The temptation of the Pastoral Council then becomes, to take this on themselves, and they forget so easily that they in turn need to involve the whole parish community as partners in whatever ways are possible and necessary.

### For the evangelisation of the world we live in

One of the dangers of religion is that it can easily become divorced from life and the two run on parallel lines. The empowerment of the laity is about bridging that gap. Christianity is not just a religion but is a whole way of life that is lived in the world of each person who professes faith in Christ. The task of the Christian is to find the appropriate ways of doing this in her/his particular circumstances. Within a parish, people can be helped in this task through courses on the social teaching of the Church and through a study of the documents of the Second Vatican Council and the many developments that have taken place since then. There is a very wide gap between what the Church teaches and most people's understanding of this teaching, a gap that can only be bridged with study and a willingness of lay Catholics to put time and effort into this.

So, the kind of questions that we have to explore together today in fresh ways are: what does it mean to be a Catholic and be in business in our world, possibly as an employer of other people? What does it mean to be a Catholic and be an employee working for a firm or in an institution? What does it mean to be a Catholic parish community and be confronted with the issues of our world of people living in poverty, people who are homeless, people who are migrants, refugees or asylum seekers, people who are travellers? What does it mean to be a Catholic parish community and see what people are doing to others through violence or war or what nations are doing to the Earth, most of which remains unchallenged? What does it mean to be a Catholic and be engaged in professions like doctor or teacher or politician? What does it mean to be a Catholic and be unemployed or having to live in poverty? There are so many questions that we would prefer to leave unasked. And yet it is vital for the health and well-being of God's Kingdom that we would pursue these together and where most of the emerging answers are coming from the laity of the Church.

5.  **The involvement of children and young people**
    We are all painfully aware of the great challenges there are for young people today in a culture that has drugs readily available, that promotes alcohol as the way to happiness, in which sex is widely encouraged as an activity for personal fulfilment, where the only really important person is oneself. We are also painfully aware of the absence of so many of our young people from the life of the Church. And there is the

challenge we have to face. We face it for two very important reasons.

Firstly, we go after the issue of involving our young people with us with a true conviction that a knowledge of Christ is the greatest gift we can give them. We find the ways of doing this, remembering that they have to grow into it and that that growth is never completed in this life. So, one of the criteria for youth ministry has to be the provision of good memories of Christ and his Church for children growing up. We have to be creative and inventive in finding all the ways possible for doing this. We need to create possibilities through which the parish community, through suitable representatives, can accompany children and young people from the time we baptise them to the time they take full responsibility for their own faith. There are particular times when we need to be especially attentive to this. When children are young, they can be included in Mass in a special way through having a Children's Liturgy of the Word. This helps them to look forward to going to Mass every Sunday and they can bring so much richness back to their homes through the work they do. When children are preparing to move from first-level to second-level education, they need special care. In Ireland most of them receive the Sacrament of Confirmation at this time. Unfortunately this Sacrament is now often cynically referred to as the Sacrament of leaving the Church. Unless we accompany them at this time they can easily get lost to us because it is such a traumatic transition in our present society. The Nazareth Programme is an excellent way of engaging with this. The years of second-level education are years when we need to be particularly attentive to our young people. They don't have the connections with the parish that they used to have. It is up to us to create new connections through some of the excellent youth programmes that are available today. And when young people move beyond second-level education and into employment or third-level education, again it is our responsibility as a community to forge the links that will help them to keep Christ at the centre of their lives, keep his way as their way, have him as the light and the hope of their lives.

We can easily look at our young people today and stand in judgement on them and complain about the awful things that

*One of the criteria for youth ministry has to be the provision of good memories of Christ and his Church for children growing up*

are happening in their kind of culture. We need to look at ourselves as a parish community and make a commitment to our young people that we will do everything possible to ensure that they need never lose the wonderful treasure of their faith and the richness of living out that faith to the full.

**We need them among us**
The second reason for putting all possible resources into the faith development of children and young people is because we need them among us. We need their energy and their sense of aliveness. Of course these qualities are disturbing at times because they can be the source of noise and confusion. And we want our young people but we also want everything to remain as it always was. We cannot have it both ways. We also need our young people with us because of their ability to question everything. This too can be very disturbing but it is a disturbance that is needed because it is only when we are asking questions that we will come to a greater knowledge of the deepest truths. One of the frequent questions that our young people ask is 'Why should I go to Mass?' Parents especially dread that question but when you look at it, isn't it a wonderful question that can lead us, not so much away from going to Mass as to being able to celebrate it with ever greater joy and enthusiasm. There are very many other questions that our young people ask that find an echo in the hearts of many of us. They are precious moments of God's grace.

*We need our children and young people with us because of the sense of hope they bring.*

We need our children and young people with us because of the sense of hope they bring. They are the only hope we have for the future of the Church we love and because of that we need to nurture them with everything we can possibly think of in the present. Investing in them is like investing in the future, something that makes admirable sense in every other sphere of life. It needs to make sense in this as well.

Children especially and our young people also give us a real sense of a new beginning. We can easily get into a mentality of growing old, coming near the end. They teach us that we are only coming near the beginning and that is the nature of the Church. A Church that lets itself grow old is not in line with the way of Christ who is risen and lives among us. No matter what age any of us is, we have a responsibility to stay young in heart and spirit. The Church has to be a wonderful adventure of transformation of our world rather than a religion that we practise with reluctance and out of fear. Children and young people are the prophets of always beginning, with all the uncertainties that brings but where the future is opening out in front of us.

However, we cannot have our young people among us and have nothing significant for them to do. A community that is worthy of the name has to be creative in finding ways for this involvement. It needs to be in terms of the worship of the community. But it also needs to be in terms of the ministry of the community to its members and to the world. Even the youngest child has gifts to bring, not in the same ways as adults bring their gifts, but just as vitally. We can easily expect young people to be adults in their sense of responsibility and commitment. It cannot happen that way. So, how can we involve children and young people according to what they bring? And how can we involve them in significant ways?

6. Marriage And Family Life

The sixth major task of every parish community is to support and develop Marriage and Family Life. First of all the relationship of married couples holds a place of special reverence in our life of faith. As Catholics, we acknowledge this relationship as one of the seven sacraments of the Church and as such we put it on a par with the other six. In all the sacraments we have a sense of receiving them. It is also true to say that we become them. For example, we don't just receive the Eucharist. The tradition of the Church is that we become what we receive, that by receiving the Body of Christ we become the Body of Christ. This is true in a special way of our married couples. They become the sacrament of marriage and as such their love for one another becomes one of the major sources of the presence of Christ in our world and one of the main ways he saves the world through his death and resurrection. Because of this all of us, whether we are married or single, religious or priest, have a serious responsibility for the health and well-being of our married couples. The community especially has pledged itself in every wedding to support each couple in every way they will need in living out their vows of love for each other.

### Sacrament of community

The married couple has a special role as prophet to all that we have been looking at here. They are firstly prophets of what it means to be a community. If the relationship is to work, they must both work at it. This is true for a healthy community also. It is only in so far as each person works at it that our community will grow into its full potential. In the couple's relationship there has to be equality but difference. This has to be true of the Christian community also. The couple have to learn to grow in partnership. Today, one of the things that is annoying is how people talk about partners rather than wife/husband. But there is a real truth in the term partner, where decisions are made together and responsibility is shared for those decisions. And how important this is in the growth of the parish community also.

### Sacrament of Ecumenism

One of the most important truths about a marriage relationship is that it is made up of two very different people. Sometimes this gets totally overlooked and the sign of a good marriage becomes where the couple can say that they are the same, they think the same way about everything, they feel the same way about everything. This is a huge mistake because it is not possible. Even if it were possible it is not a good way to be. This tension of trying to make the other person the same as you is also seen in the whole movement of Ecumenism today. In people's minds is the idea that if everyone becomes Catholic or Protestant or non-denominational then we will be one. The opposite is truly the case. It is only when each Church becomes fully itself that we can be one because then each Church will be fully built on Christ.

### Sacrament of openness to the world

On the face of it, marriage looks like it is just between two people and it is their personal affair. This is also true of how we perceive our life of faith. It is so often seen as a personal or even private thing that is only concerned with our own salvation. However, marriage cannot be lived in isolation from the world that exists around a couple. They are affected in all kinds of ways by the values and standards of that world. And they are also called by their vocation to make a difference in that world by bringing new and fresh values and standards that can show society what human life is about. In a way we could say that the purpose of marriage as an institution and as a sacrament is to transform the world into being a human family that is moving into being the kingdom of God. The Church in general has that same vocation but needs to bring the values of Christ, which are the values of love, to bear on every society. Marriage is a prophetic voice calling for this.

### Sacrament of empowerment

In marriage a couple don't just receive a sacrament. They become a sacrament. They become a living source of the presence of Christ for the salvation of the world. They live out their sacrament in and through their love for each other and it is that very love that is the deepest way for a couple to practise their faith. What is true of the married couple should also be true of every follower of Christ. Baptism is not something a person simply receives. Rather, through Baptism a person becomes a disciple of Christ with the full potential of all that this means. In Confirmation each person is commissioned to take her/his full place in the life of the Church. The problem though is that, because of the ways we think and the ways we are structured, there is very little place in the Church for every individual. This is because we have reduced the meaning of practising faith to a few actions and duties rather than finding the ways of living life to the full for the kingdom of God.

### Sacrament of new life

A phrase that is often heard in Church circles is 'keep the faith'. This is like telling a married couple 'keep your love for each other.' The reality is that most married couples long to share their love for each other with children. And it is in that very act of sharing that so many couples find their love growing. A high percentage of couples today cannot have children of their own. This is traumatic for very many. But so often they share their love by adopting a child or children and their love flourishes. This same phenomenon is true of faith in the Church. If our efforts are purely to hang on to what we have we are doomed. It is only in handing on faith to others that our own faith will grow.

However, a couple don't just have children. They become totally caught up with nurturing these children, caring for

*They become a living source of the presence of Christ for the salvation of the world.*

143

them, loving them, guiding them, working for everything that is best for them. This must be true also of our communities of faith, our parishes. If we are going to baptise infants and confirm young people then we have to be willing to invest everything in their spiritual welfare as they grow up and for the rest of their lives.

A couple who have children, either their own or adopted, will always have them, even when they have grown up and have set up their own lives. There is always a place for them at the family table. So too, a parish that accepts new life and nurtures it cannot become too demanding of people but must always ensure that there is a welcome and a place at the table for everyone. It was always a lovely characteristic of our Catholic tradition that a person doesn't have to be good to belong. We are in danger of losing this important quality when there is a demand for perfection in faith or morals.

Married couples are very important to young people. The young are always fascinated by the stories of committed love that married couples can tell. They are intrigued by the on-going sexual relationship and they are drawn by the reality that married couples speak. In dealing with our young people today our parish communities have to learn the ways of being real, of being enthusiastic, of being truthful and faithful. People often bemoan the fact that so many young people are missing from the Eucharist and from most of our gatherings. This is not necessarily all the fault of the young people. It could also be that we have not found the ways of revealing Christ to them. Those ways are there to be found by us.

### The Domestic Church
In the last few pages we have been focusing on the marriage relationship because this is a vital part of our understanding of and inspiration for our Christian way of life. We make this concentration on the sacrament of marriage while being very conscious that a married couple with children is not the only reality of family life. There are many combinations for family life today. And the wonderful truth is that all of them are sacred. Every human relationship that is founded on love is sacred and is in some way graced by God. None of them are perfect. And they don't have to be.

The family has been named the Domestic Church. This is true of the couple with children; the lone parent with children; the couple without children; a person on her/his own etc. The Domestic Church means that a primary place of the presence of God among us through Christ is our homes, through the intimate love relationships of our families. In this setting the principal way we practise our faith is through the quality of the love we have for one another. So, a husband or wife practises faith mainly through how she/he loves her/his spouse, particularly sexually. A parent practises faith by how she/he loves her/his children. And the main practice of faith for children is in their love for their parents and brothers or sisters.

*Prayer is essential so that this love can grow and expand.*

When we think of it like this we can take great encouragement from the fact that there is a lot of Christian faith being practised in almost every home. However, prayer is essential so that this love can grow and expand. And this is the bit that can be missing in many of our homes. Love is a God gift. It is too big for any of us to handle on our own. Through prayer in the family we can gain the strength to love even at times when we don't feel like it; to be faithful when we are tempted to stray; to forgive even when we are angry or hurt; to be generous even when we feel stretched by demands; to be joyful even when things are not going well; to be at peace even when there are difficulties or problems.

**The Parish Community**
The parish is a community of Domestic Churches. The main function of this community is to enable us to gather to worship God especially in the Eucharist every Sunday and, by doing this, to renew, week by week, our commitment to the way of Christ. In this Community also we commit our children to Christ through the Sacrament of Baptism; we consecrate our young people to Christ in the Sacrament of Confirmation; we claim the pain and suffering of our sick and elderly to fill out what is lacking in the sufferings of Christ by the Sacrament of Anointing; we assure the future of a living faith through the Sacrament of Matrimony and the future of the Eucharist by the Sacrament of Holy orders; and we acknowledge our sinfulness and constantly begin again joyfully in the Sacrament of Penance and Reconciliation. It is into this Community also that we bring

all our needs and where we support one another through our prayer. Worship and prayer are at the very core of what our parish community is about and that is how it must always be.

However, the real test of our worship and prayer is how these are translated into love for one another. It is so easy to become a people of rituals and to see these rituals as simply doing our duty to God. The importance of these sacred rituals is not what we are doing for God but leaving ourselves open to what God wants to do with us. And he wants us to be a people who reveal Christ to the world through how we are with one another. A parish community needs to be a place where every person can feel at home. It needs to be a setting in which every Domestic Church gets support to live the intimate relationships of love ever more fully – where married couples are helped to treasure their love and grow in it; where the single person is assured of her/his value in the plan of God; where parents are given practical support in bringing up their children; where children and young people have their gifts recognised and where openings are created for those gifts to be developed and used; where the sick and elderly are given every possible accompaniment and those who care for them do not feel abandoned; where vocations to the priesthood are promoted and where religious life is developed so that the generosity of total self-giving to others can be promoted. The parish community is a community of faith that is called to be at the service of the world around it. This needs the active participation of all who make up that community.

## 20. THE TRANSFIGURATION

*(Matthew 17:1-8)*

When we turn to the Scriptures, very often we do so to discover more fully what is in them. This is a very valid and necessary thing to do. But the Scriptures are also given to us so that we can discover what is in us, who is in us, and as a result we can become the glory of God. The Scriptures are the revelation of the deepest truths about each of us individually and of us as the Church and of us as God's beloved humanity. A story like the Transfiguration is not simply a story from the past that we can read and admire and learn something from. It is also the story of the present, it is our story into which we can enter ever more fully and because of which we can be enlivened as God's people.

*Six days later, Jesus took with him Peter and James and his brother John and led them up a high mountain where they could be alone. There in their presence he was transfigured: his face shone like the sun and his clothes became as white as the light. Suddenly Moses and Elijah appeared to them; they were talking with him. Then Peter spoke to Jesus. 'Lord,' he said 'it is wonderful for us to be here; if you wish, I will make three tents here, one for you, one for Moses and one for Elijah.' He was still speaking when suddenly a bright cloud covered them with shadow, and from the cloud there came a voice which said, 'This is my Son, the Beloved; he enjoys my favour. Listen to him.' When they heard this, the disciples fell on their faces, overcome with fear. But Jesus came up and touched them. 'Stand up,' he said 'do not be afraid.' And when they raised their eyes they saw no one but only Jesus.*

### Parish Implications

### Called by Name

There are two major mistakes that are constantly being made by us in relation to our life of faith. The first of these is that we can easily regard our faith as accidental in our lives. It just happened that I was born into this kind of family, reared in this kind of community, educated in this kind of school. It looks very much like an accident of birth and because of that can be regarded as an imposition of life. Because of seeing it like that many people today easily walk away from it and don't look back.

But even those who don't walk away can be living with this attitude to their faith. This is seen in the ways we Catholics tend to reduce the practice of faith to a bare minimum. In fact, we identify a practising Catholic as one who goes to Mass every Sunday. After that grows the demand that the Mass be as short as possible, with people at times driving a distance to get a quicker Mass than what they have in their own parish! This minimalism is destroying us because it creates the idea of our faith as a burden to be carried and we will carry it with reluctance but nevertheless it is a burden imposed on us.

*'May they all be one. Father, may they be one in us, as you are in me and I am in you, so that the world may believe it was you who sent me. I have given them the glory you gave to me, that they may be one as we are one. With me in them and you in me, may they be so completely one that the world will realise that it was you who sent me and that I have loved them as much as you loved me.' (Jn 17)*

The story of Christ's Transfiguration points to one of the deepest truths in our lives, a truth that is core to the whole Scriptural revelation, namely that our faith is not an accident but a personal call from Christ. The opening sentence of the Transfiguration story reads: 'Jesus took with him Peter, James and his brother John.' He always calls by name and the truth is that the name of each one of us has been spoken by Christ and continues to be spoken by him. We are with Christ, not as an accident of life, but on his initiative and because of the burning love he has for each one of us in his heart. Our responsibility is to say yes or no, to follow him or not. And if we follow him there are no limits, no sense of the minimum. Our faith, far from being a burden that is reluctantly carried, can become a wonderful adventure that we enter into as we are carried along by the love of God given to us in Christ.

The second major mistake in the living of our faith is that we can think of it as our own initiative. It is because I choose, I decide, I follow. This attitude is not necessarily a conscious one but can be seen in the ways we behave. When we find ourselves standing in judgement on other people or on the world we live in and condemning them we are living this attitude. We become self-righteous because we are right and anyone who does not agree with us or who lives a different way is wrong and to be condemned. We become arrogant in our self-righteousness. And arrogance should have no place in our following of Christ. Rather, if we are truly in touch with his love that gathers us to himself, we will have his compassion, his kindness, his tenderness for every person and our lives will have a quality of awesomeness at the privilege that is ours.

The attitude of faith being primarily our own initiative also shows itself in how we make it our own possession and want to

shape it in our own way. We often hear of a la carte Catholics who pick and choose the bits that suit and leave the rest aside. That is one expression of what is being said here. But a much more serious expression is seen in the many bishops and priests as well as laity who, even after almost half a century, have not responded to the vision for the Church that was given to us by the Second Vatican Council and all the wonderful developments since then. They may have changed some of the externals in the buildings but have held firmly to how things were, especially in terms of control. The Church is their possession and they make sure it's going to stay that way.

The deepest truth is clearly that faith and the Church belong to Christ and are his gifts to us as he calls us to follow him. The only questions for us are how does he want us to be? What shape does he want us to have today so that the world can know his salvation? Our responsibility is to pursue those kinds of questions, knowing that change is always called for because it is Christ we are serving and the world we are responding to.

**Five Areas of Change**

The story of the Transfiguration of Christ gives us five indications of the shape we as the Church need to have in our following of Christ for the salvation of the world.

1.  **A sense of Personal Dignity**
    By far the most sacred thing in our living of faith is the dignity of every person who is part of our community and also of every person beyond our community. The Church is not always faithful to this priority as we make other things, e.g. teachings, laws, practices, more important. The changes that have taken place over the past 40–50 years are geared to restoring this priority. We see this in the changes that have taken place in the Liturgy which has become much more person centred and people friendly. But the externals of the Liturgy can be changed while the spirit remains the same. For example, the Sunday Eucharist is a sacramental celebration of our community with one another and one of its purposes is to build our community ever more strongly. At the heart of the Eucharist is the plea that 'we may become one body, one spirit in Christ.' The reality is that we just want to say our prayers, to be left alone, to get it over as

quickly as possible, and to get away. We need to let the call of Christ move us out of that way of being and set us free to be his body. Or, another example is in how we respond to parents and children. As a Catholic people we have a great reverence for human life from the moment of conception. But then a child is born and babies cry. So often in our congregations young people don't feel free to bring their very young children to Mass because of the way they are treated by particular priests or the way they are regarded by parishioners. To get over this difficulty, some parishes have built what they call 'crying chapels', a place where parents can bring their babies and young children and the rest of the congregation is not disturbed. It might be more appropriate if those who get annoyed with babies and young children would go into the 'crying chapel' and let our worship be refreshed by new life.

The above are only a couple of examples of how we need to change far more than just the externals of our celebrations and take on a new heart of deep reverence for one another. This is true also for all the other points of celebration in our Liturgy like Baptism, Anointing of the Sick, Confirmation, Reconciliation, Marriage. The priority has to be the people. The ritual that is prescribed is at the service of people's dignity and goodness and needs to be celebrated with that firmly in mind.

2. **A sense of wonder and gladness**

*Lord, it is wonderful for us to be here.*

Peter said: 'Lord, it is wonderful for us to be here'. Every person who is baptised and confirmed among us has the right to be able to make that statement as a feature of their belonging to the Church. So often though we settle for being able to say 'it's not bad'; 'it's ok'. And this falls a long way short of 'it's wonderful'. We owe it to each other to work together to make everybody's experience of belonging to the Church a really good one. Of course this cannot happen all the time but it does need to be a significant part of our experience.

**Suspicious of joy**

An important consideration in this of course is that we often don't allow one another to be enthusiastic about the really important things in life. A good example of this is in the area of prayer. The Church has always encouraged people to pray and rightly so. Then in the 1960s/70s the Charismatic Renewal Movement became part of the Catholic Church. This movement not only helped many people to pray in new ways but actually helped them to enjoy praying. Cold water was thrown at them from all angles from bishops, priests and laity. There was almost an instinctive desire to dampen down the fire of fervour before it could run wild.

It's not only in the area of religious fervour that people are suspicious of joy and enthusiasm. Our society tolerates almost everything, except a married couple who continue to enjoy their romance with each other. If you were to see a middle aged man and woman walking along holding hands or stopping occasionally for a kiss or a cuddle you could be almost certain they are not married, at least not to each other! The expectation is that once the honeymoon is over they will settle down to being mediocre and unfortunately many couples meet this expectation.

**Building for joy**
A primary task for us as followers of Christ is to build the Church as a people of joy and gladness. The starting place for this has to be our homes where everyone in our homes – a wife, a husband; a child, a parent – can truly say 'it is wonderful to be here'. This can only happen when we are dedicating time to one another. A second gift that is essential to give to one another in our homes is affection in word and in action. If the sentence 'I love you' is a part of the daily experience in marriage and in family life there will be a lot of joy in our homes. And if this statement of love is shown to be real through touch and embrace, that sense of gladness will be greatly increased.

Another place where joy needs to be built is in the parish community. When we gather to celebrate the Eucharist or other parish events we need to deliberately choose joy as an experience we bring to one another. This is done in how we greet one another. It can be built by such simple means as a smile, a word of encouragement, a moment or two spent with someone we don't know. Everyone can contribute to that sense of well-being that needs to be a major characteristic of who we are as God's people.

3. **A sense of freedom**

Jesus came up to them (the disciples), he touched them and said: 'Stand up, do not be afraid'. In the Scriptures fear is clearly identified as the single greatest enemy to faith and love. It is said that the sentence 'do not be afraid' is used 365 times throughout the Scriptures. Whether that figure is accurate or not is not important. What is accurate is the knowledge that it is by far the most frequently spoken word of God.

**Various kinds of fear**

**Fear of Failure.** This is a fear that dictates the limits that people set to their relationships with each other and with God. We are all very conscious of our frequent failures but we don't want others to see them. So we have to pretend to be perfect. We avoid situations that could show us as less. A very simple example of this in the context of parish is when someone is asked to do a reading at Mass. The most frequent question asked is: are there any big words in it? If there are then most people will refuse to do it because they don't want to risk failure. A more serious example is in the marriage relationship of couples who don't want to get too close to each other in case the marriage ends either in the death of a spouse or the betrayal by a spouse. And so they lose one of the great opportunities of human life – a deep intimacy with the one they love.

**Fear of criticism.** One of the sad realities of parish community life is the way people talk about one another. The people who are most involved in the life of the parish are the ones who are most often unfairly criticised. Statements like who does she think she is?; look at so–and–so, up there again; your man is in everything but the Crib, and so on ensure that a lot of people will not get involved in their parish because they don't want those same things to be said about them. And so, most parishes are left with a few very generous women and men bearing the brunt of the involvement. We impose fear on one another by these kinds of criticisms. We need to root these out and replace them with affirmation so that people can have the freedom to be generous with their talents.

**Fear of being used or taken for granted.** People often refuse to get involved in their parish because they think if they do something they will be on call for everything. This is true in regard to people joining parish organisations. Often they see that if they join, the expectation is that it is a life membership. It is also true of individual actions, that one will only lead to another and they will never get out of it. And so they choose to do nothing apart from their duty. We need to free up this situation through ensuring that people are affirmed and thanked frequently for their goodness and generosity.

**Fear of what it will cost.** The cost here is not seen in monetary terms but rather in terms of time and attention and energy. This is probably the most debilitating fear of all as it runs through all the important aspects of our human lives and forces us to settle for so little in our love relationships and in our experience and knowledge of God. Everything gets measured by personal convenience and easily gets reduced to mediocrity because we want to be in control of everything and everybody including God.

We need to hear Christ constantly speaking his word to us: 'stand up, do not be afraid'. And we need to speak that word to one another in his name so that the presence of Christ can become ever more visible among us.

4. **A sense of presence**

'The disciples looked up and saw no one but only Jesus'. The problem for our life together in the Church is that we look up and see everything and everybody except Jesus!! We so easily get ourselves caught up with personalities, embroiled in issues, deflated by scandals, that we forget the real purpose and power of the whole thing – the real, living, pulsating presence of Christ among us. We owe it to one another to constantly return to this core of our faith and look at the personalities, tackle the issues and handle the scandals from there.

**How do we get in touch with Christ's presence?**

The first and most obvious way is through prayer at every level. Our own personal prayer is vitally important for the whole body of the community. We owe it to one another to develop a good form of personal prayer that keeps us in touch with Christ's presence. In this personal prayer we bring all those we love to him so that we learn to see them through his eyes. His eyes only see the goodness in each person and we have a lot to learn from him. In our personal

prayer we bring the issues that could divide us from each other to him so that we can constantly learn that no issue, no matter how important, is ever more important than another human being. And in our personal prayer we bring all the scandals to him so that we can learn gentleness in judgement and forgiveness for even the worst sins. Prayer changes us by rooting us in him.

Liturgical prayer is also a vital part of our awareness of the real presence of Christ. The celebration of Mass and all the Sacraments needs to be done in ways that reveal this awesome presence. It is so easy to get into the mentality of treating these events as ends in themselves. When we do that the Eucharist and the other sacraments become either a performance maybe for the priest or others who are taking a significant role in it or else it becomes a ritual that is done with the minimum of care. One of the main purposes of every Liturgy is to reveal Christ as present among us and everything needs to be geared towards this end.

Prayer with one another is also a very important contribution to our growing awareness of the presence of Christ with us. Prayer together in our homes helps to place him there in the Domestic Church. And prayer together when we meet in any organisation that deals with the life of the Church is vital. This should not just be a token prayer that helps to fulfil some kind of duty. It should be prayer that helps us to remember what our particular group is about – not just the work of the Lord but the Lord of the work. This prayer together is particularly important for meetings of the Parish Pastoral Council, as they represent the leadership of the parish, and any other meetings that are associated with them.

5.   A sense of purpose
**The marriage question**
Most married couples look at their relationship asking the question: Are we alright? And the answer generally is yes. They might identify a few things that could be improved on but there is no real urgency for the improvements. Of course it is the wrong question! The right question for a married couple is: How do we need to be in our relationship so that others will be alright? The 'others' are first and foremost their own children. How do they need to be so that their children

can grow up in an atmosphere of love and affection, of joy and peace, of security and generosity? That changes the focus of the relationship and the decisions that have to be made for the relationship. But the 'others' are not just a couple's own children. How do they need to be so that young couples preparing for marriage can have hope and confidence?; that the parish community may be enriched by their Sacrament of Marriage? The purpose of a couple's marriage is not just themselves but the Church and the world.

**The parish question**

What is said here about a married couple is also true of every parish. So many parish Communities do not see a need for radical renewal. At least they see some things that could be improved, but without any great urgency. The question for a parish is not: Are we alright? but rather: How do we need to be as a parish so that our children and young people growing up can have a living faith in Jesus Christ? Facing that question alone could turn the whole parish upside down. How do we need to be so that those who have left us would want to come back? Radical changes would probably be called for. How do we need to be so that those who are hurt or damaged by life, maybe through divorce or family break-up, can find a true home among us? This would demand of us to let go of the many false judgements we make of people and allow ourselves to be formed in compassion. How do we need to be so that people living among us from other countries or cultures in no way are made to feel like foreigners or strangers? This would demand of us to let go of our racial and other prejudices. How do we need to be so that those who are elderly or sick or house-bound will be well looked after and cared for and treasured? This would demand of us our time, our resources, our interest way beyond any self-interest.

**Conclusion**

The Transfiguration of Christ took place, not just for the sake of the three disciples who were there, but so that over 2000 years later we would believe in Christ. In turn, our faith is not just for ourselves and our comfort and our salvation but so that through us others can come to know Christ and put their lives in his hands. We need to grow into that sense of purpose personally and as a Community.

## 21. THE PRAYER OF JESUS AT THE LAST SUPPER

*(John 17)*

The most important truth about prayer, and one we so easily overlook, is that prayer is happening all the time. We know this from our belief in the Communion of Saints and our knowledge of the Church throughout the world. It is given particular significance by Chapter 17 of St John's Gospel. Here we have the revelation of the prayer of Jesus at the Last Supper. However it is not just a prayer spoken on one occasion but rather the continuous prayer being spoken before the throne of God. And our names are in it.

*After saying this, Jesus raised his eyes to heaven and said:*

*'Father, the hour has come; glorify your Son so that your Son may glorify you; and, through the power over all mankind that you have given him, let him give eternal life to all those you have entrusted to him. And eternal life is this: to know you, the only true God, and Jesus Christ whom you have sent.*

*I have glorified you on earth and finished the work that you gave me to do. Now, Father, it is time for you to glorify me with that glory I had with you before ever the world was. I have made your name known to the men you took from the world to give me. They were yours and you gave them to me, and they have kept your word. Now at last they know that all you have given me comes indeed from you; for I have given them the teaching you gave to me, and they have truly accepted this, that I came from you, and have believed that it was you who sent me. I pray for them; I am not praying for the world but for those you have given me, because they belong to you: all I have is yours and all you have is mine, and in them I am glorified. I am not in the world any longer, but they are in the world, and I am coming to you. Holy Father, keep those you have given me true to your name, so that they may be one like us.*

*While I was with them, I kept those you had given me true to your name. I have watched over them and not one is lost except the one who chose to be lost, and this was to fulfil the scriptures. But now I am coming to you and while still in the world I say these things to share my joy with them to the full. I passed your word on to them, and the world hated them, because they belong to the world no more than I belong to the world. I am not asking you to remove them from*

*the world, but to protect them from the evil one. They do not belong to the world any more than I belong to the world. Consecrate them in the truth; your word is truth.*

*As you sent me into the world, I have sent them into the world, and for their sake I consecrate myself so that they too may be consecrated in truth. I pray not only for these, but for those also who through their words will believe in me. May they all be one. Father, may they be one in us, as you are in me and I am in you, so that the world may believe it was you who sent me. I have given them the glory you gave to me, that they may be one as we are one. With me in them and you in me, may they be so completely one that the world will realise that it was you who sent me and that I have loved them as much as you loved me.*

*Father, I want those you have given me to be with me where I am, so that they may always see the glory you have given me because you loved me before the foundation of the world. Father, Righteous One, the world has not known you, but I have known you, and these have known that you have sent me. I have made your name known to them and will continue to make it known, so that the love with which you loved me may be in them, and so that I may be in them.'*

'In the name of the bishop they gather the family of God as a community enthusiastically striving towards unity, and lead it in Christ through the Spirit to God the Father.'
(St Cyprian)

## Parish Implications

### The real presence

The core of our Christian faith is the real presence of Christ among us. He promised to be with us to the end of time and he is always faithful to his promise. He also told us where he will be present with us: 'where two or three are gathered together in my name I am there'; 'whatever you do to even the least of my sisters and brothers you do to me'; 'if you make your home in me, I will make my home in you'. Christ then is present with us every time we are with one another. In fact he has given us the power to make him present just by being together. What an extraordinary gift! He is made present to us by the poor and those who are forgotten. He has taken up his abode in the hearts of all who believe in him.

As Catholics we also believe in the real presence of Christ in the Blessed Sacrament reserved in all our Churches. We name his presence in the Eucharist and in the Blessed Sacrament as the

Real Presence. Sometimes this naming can block us from having to honour these other ways of his real presence with us. It is not either/or. It has to be **both** in our relationship with one another **and** in the Blessed Sacrament that he is present. And in both he should be honoured. It is right to show all the signs of honour to him in the Blessed Sacrament, such as reverently genuflecting or bowing before him, or blessing ourselves as we pass a church where we know the Blessed Sacrament is reserved. At the same time it is right to honour his presence in how we treat one another with kindness, gentleness, compassion, tenderness and love.

### A living presence

When we think about the real presence of Christ in the Blessed Sacrament, we think primarily of him there to be worshipped and honoured and prayed to. And that is certainly valid. The downside of this though can be that we develop a mentality of his presence being merely passive. He is present there but he is not doing anything. In other times this gave rise to people thinking of Jesus being lonely and the reason for visiting the Blessed Sacrament was to keep him company. However, the opposite is just the case. He lives among us to keep us company because it is we who are so often lonely or isolated or in despondency or despair. His presence among us is a living, vibrant, active presence. In the Gospels we can learn what those actions of his are. The Gospels are not just an account of what Jesus did for thirty three years but also a revelation of what he is doing in the present. He taught, he preached, he healed, he forgave sin, he gave dignity to every person, he made no distinctions between people because of age or status or gender. He gave his life for the salvation of the world. And he proclaimed the reign of God. All of those actions are his today also, symbolised in his presence in the Blessed Sacrament and effected through his presence in our relationships as his Body.

### A praying presence

One of the actions of Jesus in the Gospels is that he prayed. We see him going off to a lonely place to pray. We see him bringing his disciples off by themselves to pray. And we see him praying in the company of those he taught and preached to and healed. Chapter 17 of St John's Gospel, however, is particularly important in our understanding of the praying presence of

Christ. It is given to us as the continuous prayer of Christ in the presence of God. It is called the priestly prayer of Christ. Sometimes this is mistakenly reduced to meaning his prayer for priests. This wonderful chapter of John's Gospel is the eternal prayer of Christ as priest. And it needs to become the prayer of all those who share in his priesthood through Baptism. We believe that all prayer is answered by God. How much more so can we be certain that this prayer pouring out of the heart of Christ will be answered by God. However, we also have to answer this prayer through how we live in relationship with one another and with the earth that we live in.

## A sense of direction

At the centre of this prayer of Christ is the passionate plea: 'Father, may they be one'. He repeats it over and over because ultimately this is what humanity is about, this is what all of creation is about. This plea coming from the heart of Christ impacts on us at every level of human relationships.

**'Father, may they be one': married couples.** Throughout this book we have highlighted the central importance of married couples as the completed image of God, the sign of God's love and the sacrament of Christ's relationship with his Church. Unity has to be the goal of every marriage if they are to be true to their calling.

*Community with one another is what the parish is about.*

**'Father, may they be one': each family.** The second Vatican Council identified the family as the Domestic Church. This is a primary place of the presence of Christ for our world. For this presence to be effective for salvation, unity in the family is vital. This unity is shown by how each person in the family is treasured as different and each person can feel at home.

**'Father, may they be one': the parish.** The parish is traditionally the basic unit of the Church for us as Catholics. The notion of parish is either territorial according to where people live, or personal according to choice. In either case, community with one another is what the parish is about. This community is particularly marked by how people care for one another and by how they share their possessions, material and otherwise, especially with the poor.

**'Father, may they be one': the diocese.** Parishes do not exist in isolation but as parts of the local Church of the diocese. The ordained priesthood is an extension of the pastoral call of the bishop to care for and empower all the people. Unity in the priesthood is essential for building unity in the diocese. This is so very dependent on the bishop being a pastor more than an administrator.

**'Father, may they be one': the universal Church.** Catholics identify the Pope as the visible point of unity in the Church. Maybe here especially we encounter the greatest struggle as to what unity means. Some people see it as everybody being the same and this sameness is based on what the Pope says. Of course this is a nonsense because unity has to be built on diversity, which is the very nature of being human. It is so important, within the context of our unity, that everyone is able to engage with their own questions, their own doubts and struggles, their own ways of seeing things, while being open to responding to the wisdom of others who are in a particular pastoral and leadership role.

*Ecumenism is not optional for Catholics.*

**'Father, may they be one': all Christians.** The many divisions that exist in Christianity have their origins in various historical situations. They also have their origins in the human heart. Today we are more keenly aware than ever of the vital need to heal those divisions and to move ever more fully into unity with one another in the name of Christ. Ecumenism is not optional for Catholics.

**'Father, may they be one': all of humanity.** We have often seen the world religions other than Christian as our competitors or even as our enemies. We would have thought of them as being wrong and ourselves as right because we carry with us the full truth in Christ. The prayer of Christ jolts us out of this kind of judgement and complacency into striving for unity in all the ways that are possible. They are our sisters and brothers. This same thing can be said about those who have no religion and maybe even no faith. We have often thought of them as being lost. We are called to think of them as our sisters and brothers and to treat them accordingly with love.

**'Father, may they be one': all creation.** Environmentalists are thankfully helping to make more of us aware of the duty we all have to care for the earth and to reverence all of creation. This same message can be found with deep roots in our Christian faith. All creation is God's creation and filled with God's spirit. We can easily think that the earth belongs to us. It is rather that we belong to the earth and being fully human is to be fully part of this wonderful creation of God's. At Christian funerals we commit our deceased 'to the earth from which we came' (*Roman Missal, Preface of Christian Death 4*). This can easily be interpreted as putting people in their proper place and a very lowly place. This statement however is putting the earth in its proper place, a glorious place, as part of the promise of a new heaven and a new earth.

## Building unity

This vision of unity at every level of human relationships does not easily come about. It has to be continuously worked at and built. In the letters of St. Paul and in the Acts of the Apostles three specific ways of building unity are mentioned several times. These are unity of mind, unity of heart, and unity of real affection. What do these mean and how do we work on them?

1.  **Unity of mind**
    This does not mean to have everyone thinking the same way. This is a temptation for all fundamentalists including those within the Catholic Church. Their crusade is often to insist that there is only one way to understand things and they bring this down to every detail. They can quote things from the Pope or from the Catechism or from revelations from Our Lady to prove that they are right. It is very unhealthy.

    Unity of mind means developing a common vision, a common purpose. It means looking in the same direction. Then there is room for everyone to contribute their own talents and insights and energy in moving forward to the fulfilment of the vision. For example, a married couple could have a common vision to have a very happy and healthy marriage. Both need to be committed to this so that it is not just a vague hope. The commitment is then lived out by each one contributing everything possible to the accomplishment of this vision. It will then become a reality. Another example is that of a religious order whose common vision is the care of the sick. This can easily become a vague commitment as more and more of their energy gets tied up in caring for the hospital. To renew a common vision it may be necessary to leave what they have and start again.

## Unity of heart

This means developing a predisposition towards the goodness of the other person. This is easier said than done! Criticism of one another is always much more common than praise and affirmation in human relationships. This is generally justified by saying that we are only telling the truth, and we sometimes even add: 'and the truth will set you free'. Criticism hardly ever sets anyone free but rather generally leads to the bondage of hurt and anger. Criticism is not based on the truth. It is always based on facts, except of course when it is a lie, and facts are what each of us sees about someone else. There is an old saying: 'you don't see things as they are. You see things as you are'. How true that is. If we are searchers for the truth, and as Christians we have to be, then we have to change ourselves so that we can know the truth. That change is into a unity of heart where we deliberately look for the good and acknowledge it constantly.

To develop this unity of heart we will need to forgive very often. We will need to forgive ourselves for our judgements and we will need to forgive others for their failings, often very substantial failings. We will also need to learn to make very generous allowances for others in which our expectations are not for perfection. And we will need to give up our innate desire to control others and instead set them free to be themselves.

A good example of the struggle for a unity of heart can be seen in the area of Ecumenism. All the Christian Churches have a common purpose, namely the gathering of the world into Christ. What blocks the advance of unity among the Churches is our criticism of each other or our desire to control. Forgiveness for the past and in the present has to be seriously worked at if this unity is to come about. And an on-going affirmation of one another needs to be a major feature of our relationship.

## Unity of real affection

The Marriage Encounter weekend has promoted, and may even have created, a very important insight for the marriage relationship that is completely transferable to all relationships: **Love is a decision.** Love is not dependent on how we feel at any particular time, although our feelings enable or hinder us from making the decision to love. We can say the same about affection. Like the word love, we so easily think immediately of feeling affectionate or not when we hear the word affection. It is a decision that we can make at any time, a decision to behave in an affectionate way towards each other whether in marriage or family life, in parish or diocesan life, in our relationships with other Christians or people of other religions or none, or in our relationship with creation. When we are living by true affection we can be certain that we will not manipulate or try to control the other.

**Different starting points, same process**

The various human relationships that are mentioned here can have different starting points. The process, however, is the same, namely to involve all three ways of building unity. For married couples, for example, the obvious starting point for their relationship is their love and affection for one another. In most marriages, apart from cultures that would have arranged marriages, this love and affection is the primary reason they decided to get married in the first place. And it is this love and affection that has to continue to sustain and nourish their marriage. The weakness of the marriage relationship is most often to be found in a lack of a clear common purpose to which they are each committed and consequently they drift along to the detriment of their love and affection, or they get into a habit of criticism or putting each other down, which of course has a very bad effect on the quality of their love. These are the two that a married couple need to work on most because it is through these that their love and affection are increased.

Family life has its starting point in unity of heart – as they say, blood is thicker than water. The weakness of family life is to be found in the other two, where there is a diminished sense of purpose in taking on responsibility for the health and well-being of the family or where affection between brothers and sisters and parents has not been developed. The lack of these two causes a lessening of the sense of belonging. Conversely, the sense of belonging is strengthened when these two are being attended to.

All the other relationships, many of which have their starting point in the first one, namely a sense of a common purpose, follow the same principle. The main reason for being together can only be strengthened to energise us when the other two are being worked on.

### John 17 – a source of hope
This extraordinary chapter of St John's Gospel gives us the knowledge that Christ is present among us, in a variety of ways, praying for us all the time. 'I pray, not only for these but for those also who through their words will believe in me.' Right through the generations of the Church our names were included in his prayer. We now are the people who have come to him through the love of those who have gone before us. And now Christ is praying in us for those who will come after us. We have a great responsibility to let ourselves go to his prayer and do all we can to build the Church in ways that will be worthy of future generations. When we look at the present and think about the future, we can easily despair. Because of Christ we can look and think with a great sense of hope. Of course we have to be greatly concerned about the present and the future. But our real concern has to be to shape the Church today through true collaboration so that it can pass into ready hearts.

'Father, I want those you have given me to be with me where I am so that they may always see the glory you have given me before the foundation of the world.' This is another very striking sentence from Christ's prayer because it is about us. Because of this we can look ahead with confidence to our own destination and we can assure that same exciting destination for all those we love.

### John 17 – A sense of adventure
'With me in them and you in me, may they be so completely one that the world may believe it was you who sent me and that I have loved them as much as you loved me.'

The adventure of our Christian calling is captured in this part of Christ's prayer. It is an adventure towards one another. However it does not close us in on one another. Rather, the test of true unity is in how much this unity opens us out beyond ourselves. Again, we can look at this in all the various relationships we have considered in this chapter. A married couple are called to love each other so much that it opens them to new life, not just by having children – or more children– but to spending their love in the service of others. Families are to love one another to the extent that hospitality becomes a feature of our homes. The parish is to build its unity to the extent where the stranger and the poor will find a true home. The unity of the diocese is to be such that it shares its resources with others in need. And the universal Church, gathered around our Holy Father, witnesses through its unity that every human person is to be reverenced deeply and that no one is to be overlooked. And as we gather the whole of humanity and all of creation into this unity that is the prayer of Christ, we aim that every woman, man, and child would come to know the wonderful love that God has for them and that Christ loves them as much as the Father loves him.

## 22. THE COMMISSIONING OF THE DISCIPLES

### (Matthew 28:16-20)

This short passage is tucked away at the end of St Matthew's Gospel, almost like a summary. In it are contained some of the most important elements of our Christian faith in terms of its origin and purpose. We here look at some of the significant words and phrases that are in it.

*'Jesus wants every human person to know him and to experience his amazing love.'*

*Meanwhile the eleven disciples set out for Galilee, to the mountain where Jesus had arranged to meet them. When they saw him they fell down before him, though some hesitated. Jesus came up and spoke to them. He said, 'All authority in heaven and on earth has been given to me. Go, therefore, make disciples of all the nations; baptise them in the name of the Father and of the Son and of the Holy Spirit, and teach them to observe all the commands I gave you. And know that I am with you always; yes, to the end of time.'*

### Parish Implications

The disciples went to **the mountain**… The image of the mountain is a very important one as we think about the ongoing renewal of the Church today. We often look for easy fixes or instant success. Or we hope that something will happen, or that someone will come along to make everything right. You can see this longing lived out when a diocese is in the process of getting a new bishop or a parish looking forward to a new parish priest. The hope is that the new person will be the solution to all our problems. And it never works out that way! We have to be the solution of all our problems. But we cannot do that without climbing the mountain.

The first thing about climbing a mountain is that it is a very deliberate action. It never happens by accident but by design. We have to set out to do it. You decide that this is where you are going and you hold to that decision.

The second thing is that it takes personal commitment of time and energy to be part of the climb. This is often what people are not willing to give for the renewal of the Church in their parish.

Climbing a mountain also demands perseverance. You don't give up at the first hurdle, and there are going to be many of those on the way. At times you may have to stop and renew your energy but even then you keep your eye on the summit.

Mountain climbing is also a team effort in which each person has a special place and to which each one brings their own gifts and expertise. The safety and well-being of the whole team depends on each individual playing her/his part fully.

And you know that when you get to the summit it will have been more than worth all the effort you have put into it. From there you will have a different vision of life, a fresh energy that comes from clear priorities and a new heart that encompasses the world.

…where Jesus had **arranged** to meet them: one of the most serious temptations for men and women is to try to be in control of everything in their lives. This extends even to trying to control God. Living a life of faith means letting go of this and allowing ourselves to be led by God's Spirit and be formed by Christ's promise. He has arranged to meet us, firstly, in the company of one another – 'where two or three are gathered together in my name, there am I in the midst of them' (Mt. 18:20). What an extraordinary arrangement that is. Every time we are with one another we make Christ present through our company with one another and we meet him there. Of course the serious implication of this is that we are always walking on sacred ground when we are with one another.

Christ has also arranged to meet us in the poor and oppressed and those who are marginalised – 'whatever you do to the least of my sisters or brothers you do to me' (Mt. 25:40). Christ is not saying that some people are better than or less than others. He is recognising the reality that in our eyes and our esteem some people are better and some lesser to us. In fact there may even be people whom we judge as having no claim at all on our love and reverence. It is the real presence of Christ we are dealing with here and a lot of change of attitude and behaviour is called for. We are in constant touch with Christ in and through our daily contacts with one another.

As Catholics we believe that Christ has arranged to meet us in and through all the Sacraments of the Church. This is especially marked by us through our reverence for the Blessed Sacrament reserved in all our churches. It is a wonderful gift of God's love but it cannot be seen in isolation from the other flesh and blood places of his presence.

And Christ has arranged to meet us in the depth of our own hearts – 'if you love me, you will keep my word and my Father will love you, and we shall come to you and make our home with you' (Jn 14:23).

**They fell down before him, though some hesitated**
In some translations this read: 'they all hesitated' which would be more in line with our own experience. There are many reasons for people's hesitations in their following of Christ. For some it is a true sense of awe at the presence of Christ and the wonder of being called. For others it can be a sense of inadequacy. For others again it can be the kinds of fear that are spoken about in the previous chapter, especially the fear of what it is going to cost us if we take the following of Christ seriously. Whatever the reason for hesitation or reluctance or doubt we don't have to worry because we are in very good company. The first disciples were just like us.

**Jesus came up and spoke to them. He said, 'All authority in heaven and on earth has been given to me'.**
The first thing Jesus does for his disciples and for us today is to establish clearly who he is. There is a strong echo here of Peter's

response to the question Jesus asks at Caesarea Philippi: 'who do you say I am? You are the Christ the Son of the living God.' This is dealt with at length on page 118 ff. The very core of our Christian faith is the person of Jesus. Everything else emanates from that core and returns to that core. It is very easy to let other things, other people, take over that core and the living of our faith gets focused on them. We have to constantly restore Christ to the centre both at a personal level and as a Church.

It is also a temptation to live as if all authority in heaven and on earth has been given to us. Authority belongs to Christ. The only authority we have as the Church is that of a messenger. Our responsibility is to be true to the message that has been given to us.

### The five commands of Christ

Having established who he is, Christ then gives his disciples his five commands. These commands are for the Church of all times and they need to be the basis for how the Church at every level lives its life.

1. **Go**
   This is his first and most essential command. It is a very dynamic word. Go forward, move, change from where you are. Our tendency can be **to stay**. Our temptation is to keep things as they are, to batten down the hatches. That is not the way of Christ. Or our mentality can be **to wait**, take it easy, don't rush things. That is not the way of Christ. Or again some people want to **go back**, to get back to the way things were, to return to the good old days, and then everything will be well again. That is not the way of Christ.

   The Second Vatican Council caught the spirit of this first command when it described the Church as a Pilgrim People. For a long time before the Council the Church was thought of as a static reality where everything was fixed and nothing much changed. The image of a Pilgrim People is just the opposite as it presents us to ourselves as a people who are always on the move and, because of that, change is constant and essential.

However, a Pilgrim People is not the same as a Wandering People. A Pilgrim People has a definite destination. It may take a long time to get there but everything is geared towards that destination. The next three commands of Christ give us a clear vision of what that destination is.

2. **Make disciples of all the nations**

This is Jesus' version of *Think Big!* It is almost like he is thinking, as he looks at his hesitant disciples, I will give them something worth worrying about. The kind of Jesus that we invent in the Church is one who, when he saw the disciples hesitating, would have said: don't worry, take your time, take it easy. Just when you are ready you might like to try this out in one of the villages nearby and then, when you are ready, you might move on to another village. The real Jesus commands us to set our sights on the horizon, to think of the very last person to hear Christ's Good News, and everything we do is leading us to that person.

Jesus wants every human person to know him and to experience his amazing love. He wants every human person to hear the call to be a disciple of his. We work towards that vision by making it worthwhile for people to be with us. That very often demands change on our part. This change sometimes involves personal change as we set out to be more attractive people, more welcoming, more hospitable. At other times it calls for parish changes as we become more involved with one another in building the parish as a place where every person can find a home and can be at home. This is the major task of the Parish Pastoral Council. It can only be done in so far as its members remember what they are about, namely to involve others in involving others.

3. **Baptise them in the name of the Father, and of the Son, and of the Holy Spirit**

All the people in our parishes are already baptised so can we approach this command of Christ as only referring to the next generation? Many parishes put a lot of effort into helping parents to prepare for the baptism of their children. And this is very good as it is often an occasion for the parents and others to renew their own baptismal promises and begin again to lead their Christian life more fully.

However, this command is not just about bringing people to the sacramental ritual of baptism. It is a call to flood this world with the love of God. It is a challenge to build our parishes in ways that people will flock to our doors looking for baptism for themselves and their children because they will want what we have. And the only way to accomplish this is to renew our own faith in the Father, the Son and the Holy Spirit.

### Into the Father

Renewing our faith in God, who is our Father, and also our Mother, is to learn to live with every person as a sister or brother. It is to grow in a real conviction of the goodness of every person and to live that conviction in our communities. It is also to grow in an awareness of the goodness of all creation and to care intensely for the earth that is our present home. It is to change radically our way of seeing things and living life. We can no longer think of our faith as just a religion with some practices through which we can please God. It is rather a complete way of life in which we are aware of God's presence in everything and consequently we know that we are always walking on holy ground. Our sacraments, our prayers, and our rituals are all moments when we renew this faith and through which we live out our baptism ever more fully. They are also moments when we thank God for all the wonders of life and ask for God's blessing on all that we desire.

### Into the Son

To renew our faith in God the Son is to let ourselves go to the truth that Christ has transformed the world, is transforming the world and will transform the world. It doesn't look like that most of the time. We are only too aware of all the problems in the Church and all the serious confusion in the world. However, through the humanity of Christ the whole of creation has been gathered into the divine life of God and there is being slowly and gradually moulded into God's kingdom, Jesus Christ. Because of this knowledge of faith we have a responsibility to be a people of hope. This hope is not just a vague desire that things might turn out all right but a confidence that they will. The true follower of Christ will be found at the heart of all human efforts to build a better and more just society where

everyone can come to know how much she/he is loved and treasured.

**Into the Holy Spirit**

To renew our faith in God, the Holy Spirit, is to take onto ourselves all the gifts of the Spirit and to release them in our communities. In every one of our parishes there are many people who possess these gifts – they have been confirmed among us. It's just that often we have to look for these people in some unexpected places. Where, for example, do we look for the gift of wisdom among us? Many of our older people live by this gift and yet how seldom are they seen as more than people in need. Or where do we look for the gift of understanding? Parents of children may be one of our main sources but we would hardly think of looking there. And so on with the other gifts of the Spirit, we have a treasure that is largely unclaimed among our people.

As we release the power of the Spirit's gifts among the parishioners, the challenge is also to live by the fruits of the same Spirit, especially in the gatherings of the parish community. St. Paul describes those fruits of the Spirit in a beautiful way in his Letter to the Galatians as follows: 'What the Spirit brings is love, joy, peace, patience, kindness, goodness, trustfulness, gentleness, and self-control' (Gal. 5, 22). If we ever want to know what a parish community should look like we have the picture there. The task is to build parishes in ways that those qualities of life are what those who live among us and around us see and experience. We will be known then as a baptised community to the glory of God.

4.  **Teach them to observe all the commands I gave you**

    To teach is the fourth command of Christ. In the Church we often make it the first and that is always a mistake. People can best learn or be taught when they feel at home and want to be there. Another mistake we can easily make with this command is to identify his commandments with rules and regulations. In the Gospels Jesus makes it very clear what his commandments are. First of all he tells us that he has not come to do away with the Law or the prophets but to fulfil them. That should be some consolation to those who wonder what ever happened to the Ten Commandments. They are still very much in place but now in Christ they are to be observed in a very different way – the way of love – because Christ also said that the whole Law and the Prophets too are summed up in the commandments 'you must love the Lord, your God, with your whole heart, your whole soul, your whole mind and your whole strength. And you must love your neighbour as yourself'. That is a very big way of living and often far beyond the limits we set to our lives. And yet that is precisely what we stand for as followers of Christ today and that is the central message that we as Christians bring to the world.

*This is a very big way of living.*

Another commandment that Christ gives us is: 'love your enemies; do good to those who harm you; pray for those who persecute you'. Again, this is a very big way of living that brings us far beyond settling for rules and regulations that we can easily control. Jesus doesn't say we shouldn't have enemies. That would be unreal in human life. And the word of Christ is always firmly rooted in human experience. He does show us a very new way to deal with one another that needs to become the way of life that is taught in our parish communities.

Right through the Gospels Christ gives his disciples other commandments. All of them are about relationships with one another and with him like, 'do not judge and you will not be judged' or 'do not store up treasures for yourselves on earth', or 'follow me' and so on. They are never commandments that are aimed purely at personal perfection but at the perfecting of our community one with one another as his Body.

Christ's final commandment given to us in the Gospels is: 'Do this in memory of me'. He gave us this commandment at the Last Supper after he had given himself to his disciples under the form of bread and wine for the first time. The Eucharist is to be at the very centre of our communities and we are called into it, not just as spectators but as participants. It was in that same setting that Christ gave us his ultimate command, 'Love one another as I have loved you'. That is the core of the way of life of the Church.

5. **Know that I am with you always,**
   **yes to the end of time**
   This fifth command of Christ is what holds all the others
   together. We have to keep returning to the core of our faith
   which is the real presence of Christ among us. When we lose
   sight of this presence of his we easily go astray. For example
   in moving forward we can become involved in crusades of
   one kind or another and those can never be what we are
   about. When we lose sight of the presence of Christ we can
   easily turn the Church into some kind of business or
   conveyor belt; or we can reduce Baptism to a ritual; or we can
   impose laws that are a burden on people's shoulders.

   One of the most important implications of Christ present
   among us is that no issue, no matter how important it is, is
   ever more important than the individual person. This can
   lead to a lot of messy situations and our tendency is to try to
   have everything in good order. It means creating room for
   every person in ways in which everyone can feel at home.
   One of the major tasks of the Church in every parish is to
   constantly find ways of helping each one to know how much
   she or he is treasured. No one person can do that, which is
   why collaborative ministry is so essential. But, equally, no
   Parish Pastoral Council can do that unless they see that their
   primary role is to involve others who, in turn, will involve
   others so that everyone in the parish is provided with the
   opportunity of serving Christ. The Parish Pastoral Council
   can become more controlling and 'clerical' than any priest
   has ever been. When that happens they have lost sight of
   what it is about, the real, living, pulsating presence of Christ
   among his people for the salvation of the world.

Glory be to the Father
and to the Son
and to the Holy Spirit.
As it was in the beginning,
is now,
and ever shall be,
world without end.
Amen.